LEADERSHIP FOR EXCELLENCE

*Insights of National School Library Media
Program of the Year Award Winners*

EDITED BY

JO ANN CARR

FOR THE AMERICAN ASSOCIATION OF SCHOOL LIBRARIAN

AMERICAN LIBRARY ASSOCIATION
CHICAGO 2008

Jo Ann Carr is director of the Center for Instructional Materials and Computing at the School of Education at the University of Wisconsin–Madison. Her research interests have focused on information literacy and curriculum materials centers. She is the editor of *Management of Curriculum Materials Centers for the 21st Century: The Promise and the Challenge*. Carr chaired the 2004–2005 National School Library Media Program of the Year Committee. In 1989, she was named the Educational and Behavioral Sciences Section Librarian of the Year. Carr earned her master's degree in library science at Indiana University–Bloomington.

While extensive effort has gone into ensuring the reliability of information appearing in this book, the publisher makes no warranty, express or implied, on the accuracy or reliability of the information, and does not assume and hereby disclaims any liability to any person for any loss or damage caused by errors or omissions in this publication.

The paper used in this publication meets the minimum requirements of American National Standard for Information Sciences—Permanence of Paper for Printed Library Materials, ANSI Z39.48-1992.

Library of Congress Cataloging-in-Publication Data

Leadership for excellence : insights of National School Library Media Program of the Year Award winners / edited by Jo Ann Carr for the American Association of School Librarians.

    p. cm.
    Includes bibliographical references and index.
      ISBN-13: 978-0-8389-0961-4 (alk. paper)
      ISBN-10: 0-8389-0961-2 (alk. paper)
    1. National School Library Media Program of the Year Award. 2. School libraries—Awards—United States. 3. Media programs (Education)—Awards—United States. 4. School libraries—United States—Case studies. 5. Media programs (Education)—United States—Case studies. I. Carr, Jo Ann. II. American Association of School Librarians.
    Z675.S3L3835 2008
    027.8—dc22

              2008000976

ISBN-13: 978-0-8389-0961-4

Printed in the United States of America

12 11 10 09 08   5 4 3 2 1

contents

preface

Since 1963, exemplary school library media programs have been honored by the National School Library Media Program of the Year (NSLMPY) Award given annually by the American Association of School Librarians. This award, sponsored by Follett Library Resources, recognizes programs that demonstrate leadership in the field and serve as models of exemplary implementation of the principles and guidelines established for the profession. The award was sponsored by Encyclopedia Britannica until 1995.

All of the school library media programs recognized during the first five years of the twenty-first century have outstanding leaders who have developed programs that are fully integrated into their local curriculum. This integration ensures that students and staff are effective users of ideas and information. In this book, these leaders provide reflections on the ways in which their programs demonstrate the basic principles of collaboration, leadership, and technology to support dynamic, student-centered library media programs. Essential to the success of these programs is a defined mission and vision that integrates school library media programs with the mission of the school or district. The focus of their programs is on building partnerships for learning through support of learning and teaching, information access and delivery, and program administration. The impact of these programs is extended to their communities through advocacy and public relations activities.

Each of these leaders exemplifies the multiple characteristics needed to build school library media programs that meet the NSLMPY criteria. These elements include the ability to reflect on one's work in order to understand what leads to success. This reflective quality is a key part of the work of the NSLMPY winners since 1963. Embracing the multiple roles of the school library media specialist as a teacher, instructional partner, information specialist, and program administrator is also part of the vision for student-centered teaching and learning, the goal of exemplary school library media programs and their leaders. Passion, enthusiasm, and creativity are hallmarks of school library media leaders. Nevertheless, these elements do not lead to success without a commitment to collaborative action with other members of the school community.

As have many members of the NSLMPY Awards Committee, I recognized that the opportunity to examine these exemplary programs is an extremely valuable professional development experience. This book now provides all library media specialists, library media educators, teachers, teacher educators, and administrators the opportunity to examine these programs.

JO ANN CARR

acknowledgments

Thanks to KeliAnn Trowbridge, Allen Ford, and Dawn Sulok for their assistance in the preparation of this manuscript.

This book is dedicated to the extraordinary school library media specialists who have engaged in the leadership and critical reflection necessary to apply for the National School Library Media Program of the Year honor. Their work serves as an inspiration for all who are committed to demonstrating the critical role of quality school library media centers in preparing the next generation of American leaders.

Finally, I offer my deep appreciation to Follett Library Resources for making it possible to recognize the work of inspirational school library media specialists.

CHAPTER 1

A Vision of Leadership

While we are busy, in fact in full swing at this time of year, we did share with one another as we looked at our program and felt renewed.[1]

The entire [NSLMPY] process, from start to finish, was the single most effective program improvement process the library media department has ever undertaken.[2]

These statements by contributors to this book echo the opinion, frequently expressed by their fellow winners of the National School Library Media Program of the Year (NSLMPY) Award, that a critical examination of their school library media programs is essential to success. This critical examination identifies not only *what* works but also *why* these strategies work.

This analysis demonstrates Lankford's essential element of leadership: the ability to ask, "Why?"[3] This ability to be reflective about the reasons for program success is demonstrated in the contributions of NSLMPY winners profiled in this book. These individuals offer their insights about their programs and provide practical, proven strategies for driving excellence within the learning community.

The roles and responsibilities of the school library media specialist that were outlined in AASL's 1998 publication *Information Power* are teacher, instructional partner, information specialist, and program administrator.[4] The library media specialist as teacher brings multiple knowledge bases to instructional design, teaching and learning styles, information literacy, and information resources to meet the needs of learners. The library media specialist as instructional partner takes a wider view of the curriculum of the school or district to integrate information literacy skills into the values of the school or district. The library media specialist as information specialist expands the range of content and process knowledge of the education community through careful identification and selection of information resources. And the library media specialist as program administrator is both a manager of processes and a mentor for library staff.

All of these roles require leadership skills. As a teacher, the school library media specialist must lead in curriculum development; as an instructional partner, the school library media specialist leads in both collaborative planning and staff development; as an information specialist, the school library media specialist has the leadership responsibility for identifying resources that meet the learning needs of the school community; and as a program administrator, the school library media specialist must show leadership in developing finance and budgeting activities, facilities management, program organization, leadership and management of library staff and volunteers, and public relations.

Wilson and Lyders have defined *leadership* as "a quality of influencing others through a sharing of vision, a respect for individual goals, an ability to build consensus, and collaborative work towards mutual purpose."[5] These roles of vision, mutual goals, consensus building, and working collaboratively are an integral part of the role of the school library media specialist. Being able to fulfill these roles requires that these specialists have the ability to communicate these with administrators and colleagues.

Effective communication with administrators enables school library media specialists to fulfill all other leadership roles. Effective communicators are

- ➤ consistent
- ➤ thorough
- ➤ timely
- ➤ observant
- ➤ appropriate
- ➤ clear
- ➤ willing to compromise
- ➤ articulate
- ➤ assertive
- ➤ savvy[6]

As these qualities demonstrate, school library media specialists must know their message; understand the needs, values, and processes of their school or district; and see themselves as part of the educational team. As part of the educational team, school library media specialists need to demonstrate their identity as teachers in many ways. Whether other teachers in the school accept the teacher role of the school library media specialist may hinge on something as subtle as the difference in the use of the word *we* versus *them* when referring to teachers.[7]

The role of instructional partner can enable the school library media specialist to be identified as a school leader.[8] In this capacity they must serve as collaboration leaders among instructional staff to ensure that information literacy and resource-based teaching can be fully used to support student achievement.

This leadership role in collaboration is necessary in part because most teacher and 71 percent of administrator education programs do not include the opportunity to collaborate with school library media programs or include information on the role of the school library media specialist.[9] The school library media specialist must also overcome the preconceptions of school administrators whose own educations did not include experiences with school library media centers as full instructional partners.[10] Former American Association of School Librarians president Barbara Stripling recognizes that the principles of *Information Power* have not become part of the education community because teacher education and administrator education programs do not "cover what a library program should be, could be, would do."[11]

Communication of the instructional leadership role of the school library media specialist needs to be based not only on an understanding of the roles outlined in *Information Power* but also must be matched by a vision of the application of these roles to the needs of the individual school or district.

This ability to effectively communicate this vision to the school or district administration is essential to the ability of school library media specialists to demonstrate leadership beyond the school library media center. It is the principal who determines which staff members serve on committees within and outside the school or district.[12]

Leadership beyond the school library media center is a common characteristic of the school library media specialists in NSLMPY-recognized programs. The school library media specialists who tell their stories in the following pages have led their principals from the role of tourists in the library media center to fully engaged citizens in a learning community committed to collaboration for student achievement.[13]

NOTES

1. Sharon Coil to J. Linda Williams, February 6, 2006.
2. Donna Helvering, "Millard Public Schools, 2003 NSLPY [*sic*] Winner," unpublished document, 2006.
3. Mary Lankford, *Leadership and the School Librarian: Essays from Leaders in the Field* (Worthington, OH: Linworth Publishing, 2006), 9.
4. American Association of School Librarians, "Roles and Responsibilities of the School Library Media Specialist," in *Information Power: Building Partnerships for Learning* (Chicago: American Library Association, 1998).
5. Patricia Potter Wilson and Josette Anne Lyders, *Leadership for Today's School Library: A Handbook for the School Library Media Specialist and the School Principal* (Westport, CT: Greenwood Press, 2001), 3.
6. Rolf Erikson and Carolyn Markuson, *Designing a School Library Media Center for the Future* (Chicago: American Library Association, 2001), 9.
7. Ruth Toor and Hilda K. Weisburg, *New on the Job: A School Library Media Specialist's Guide to Success* (Chicago: American Library Association, 2007), 13.
8. Keith Curry Lance, "Five Roles for Empowering School Librarians" (paper presented at the Annual Conference of the American Library Association, Chicago, June 23–29, 2005).
9. Gary Hartzell, "Why Should Principals Support School Libraries?" *ERIC Digest,* 2002. ERIC Document Reproduction Service ED470034, p. 2. Wilson and Lyders, *Leadership for Today's School Library,* 20.
10. Gary Hartzell, "What Does It Take?" in *The White House Conference on School Libraries Proceedings, June 4, 2002* (Washington, DC: Institute of Museum and Library Services, 2002), 27.
11. Beverly Goldberg, "Why School Libraries Won't Be Left Behind," *American Libraries* 36, no. 8 (September 2005): 41.
12. Hartzell, "Why Should Principals Support School Libraries?"
13. The concept of the principal as tourist was introduced by David V. Loertscher, "How Administrators Can Evaluate School Libraries," in *The Whole School Library Handbook,* edited by Blanche Woolls and David V. Loertscher (Chicago: American Library Association, 2005), 154.

CHAPTER 2

Leadership in Learning and Teaching

L eadership in teaching and learning can occur at many levels as the school library media specialist works within an instructional partnership to develop and implement school district standards and grade-level objectives, as well as curriculum and lesson plans for individual classes. Teaching and learning take place in both formal classroom settings and one-on-one instruction. Success as a teacher in all of these areas is dependent on collaboration in which the library media specialist works closely with other teachers to co-plan, co-teach, and co-assess student learning.[1]

This success of the collaboration depends on the quality of the relationship. Collaborative relationships must be based on respecting differences, recognizing common goals, understanding the role of each party, and commitment to continual growth of the collaboration. Six factors are important for successful collaboration:

- ➤ Environmental factors: What is the history of the collaborative partners? How does the local organizational and social climate support collaboration?
- ➤ Membership factors: Who should be members of the collaboration team?
- ➤ Process factors: Do collaborators understand their role in the collaboration and understand the process for decision making?
- ➤ Communication factors: Are opportunities for open communication most likely to be available through formal or informal means or in a combination?
- ➤ Purpose: Do collaborators share the same purpose and objectives?
- ➤ Resources: What resources are available for collaboration?[2]

In addition to the differences in subject expertise that school library media specialists and teachers bring to the collaborative process, there may also be differences in the teaching styles among teachers within a school or district. School library media specialists and their collaborative partners may be concrete sequential (step by step, get the facts), abstract sequential (inventive, logical, access to experts), abstract random (group activities, broad guidelines), or concrete random (experimenting, risk taking) in their thinking patterns. School library media specialists should identify their own teaching and learning styles. When they are collaborating with other teachers, they should consider how their instructional partner likes to learn, how they learn best, and what communication and learning tasks pose challenges for them. Knowledge of these differences will enable the school library media specialist to adapt communication to the needs of her partner, providing a group-structured environment for concrete sequential learners and respecting the intuitive, independent style of concrete random learners.[3]

The collaboration journey with an individual teacher often begins with a single step when the school library media specialist invites the classroom teacher to collaborate. Flexibility in scheduling planning time, the second critical step, demonstrates the school library media specialist's commitment to the instructional partnership. The specialist must stay involved in the development of the unit so that students benefit from the integration of the knowledge and skills that each member of the collaborative team brings to the unit. This integration should be based on shared responsibilities in the development of materials, teaching, and assessment. Following the collaboration, the school library media specialist can again exhibit the leadership skill of "why" by inviting the classroom teacher and students to look at what worked and what needs to be improved. The school library media specialist should then prepare for the next invitation by saving the lesson and the lessons learned as a starting point for the next collaboration.[4]

The collaboration journey on schoolwide issues can also be approached through specific steps. The school library media specialist should work to be on the school's curriculum committee, where her broad knowledge of the school's curriculum can be of great value. School library media center policies are important to all other areas and all members of the school's community, so the school library media specialist should involve the principal and other key leaders in their development. The goals of the school library media center should support the goals of the school, and involvement of the principal and other leaders in their development are important for ensuring this integration.[5]

Although an understanding of potential steps in collaboration is important, school library media specialists should heed the words of Norman Webb and Carol Doll, evaluators of the Library Power Program: "Collaboration is a style, not a strictly delineated procedure. Collaboration mandates personal and reciprocal contact between the individuals involved."[6] The collaboration style can and should be demonstrated in both informal and formal ways: knowing the names of all the teachers in your school; regarding hallway greetings as a conversation starter; moving around the school; sending fliers to teachers' mailboxes; asking for discussion and presentation time at grade-level meetings, departmental meetings, and faculty meetings; and serving on committees.[7]

School library media programs recognized by NSLMPY understand the cultural change required for schools to become collaborative teaching and learning environments. These programs' participation in collaborative programs has developed over time and has grown from an environment of respect that begins with an understanding of shared and complementary roles, based on a commitment to student achievement, that school library media specialists and their instructional partners share.

In this chapter, Maggie Schmude, Marilyn Cobb, and Angela Burns describe how New Trier High School's school library media specialists have worked with teachers to adapt a schoolwide assignment to multiple needs within the school. Julie Hyde-Porter and Anna Maria Menza provide two illustrations of the leadership and collaboration fostered through participating in Advanced Placement training directed to teachers in social studies. Initial collaborative teaching at New Trier is reviewed in Judy Gressel's account of work with freshman students.

Carolyn Kirio has demonstrated responsiveness to the varying needs of classroom teachers through her work in scaffolding information literacy throughout the Kapolei High School that builds on K–8 curriculum. Districtwide collaborative planning and the role it has played in promoting the role of the school library media specialist is richly detailed by a group of school library media specialists from the Hilliard City School District: Susie Alexander, Liz Deskins, Terry Lord, Marsha Pfahl, and Christina H. Dorr. Patricia Pickard of the DeKalb County (Georgia) School District describes its successful approach to districtwide planning. Another illustration of the design process at the elementary level is provided by Sharon Brubaker of H. M. Brader Elementary School.

The collaboration that Katherine Lowe describes begins with recognition by the teachers in her school of the importance of expertise in keyword searching. Another inspiring program of the DeKalb County (Georgia) School District, the Helen Ruffin Reading Bowl, demonstrates the impact of one former school library media specialist on creating a program that has grown from one school to a statewide impact. In "Power Readers" Katherine Lowe describes another collaborative program to encourage and celebrate reading.

An additional instructional leader role of the school library media specialist in staff development is described by Sharon Coil, Katherine Lowe, and Patricia Pickard.

Advanced Placement Junior Theme

MAGGIE SCHMUDE
NEW TRIER HIGH SCHOOL—WINNETKA CAMPUS, WINNETKA, ILLINOIS

SUMMARY

The Advanced Placement Junior Theme is a yearlong reading/thinking/writing project that is the result of extensive collaboration between four New Trier Advanced Placement teachers and two librarians. This team develops a list of topics and, for each topic, selects a required book, and a list of other related books, and students choose a topic from this list. The list includes topics such as America's Role in the World, The American Family, Race, Class, American Women, The Power of Place, Illness and Wellness, The Individual and Democracy, The Frontier, and Religion in America. Students must read the required book for their topic and, over the course of the year, an additional four to six books (both fiction and nonfiction); keep a research journal; and post entries concerning their reading on the class Blackboard site.

The teachers begin by showing the students how to analyze the argument that each book puts forth. The librarians teach them how to keep the research journal and how to use a graphic organizer to draw together the similarities among the books they are reading. They also help students choose books, provide a database of book reviews, and comment on the students' Blackboard postings. Later in the process, using another graphic organizer, the librarians teach the students how to develop essential questions about their topics and turn those essential questions into a thesis statement. Still later, using a website developed for this project, the librarians teach various resources that the students can use to fill the holes in their arguments: reference materials, databases, and websites. The librarians work closely and individually with both the teachers and students to help them complete their final project: a thoughtful paper with an original argument that is well supported by facts.

OBJECTIVES

The major objectives of this project are to teach students how to recognize and create strong arguments supported by fact and to incorporate those arguments into a well-written research document. The school's motto is, "Minds to inquiry, hearts to compassion, and lives to the service of humanity." This project certainly supports "minds to inquiry."

SCHOOL LIBRARY MEDIA SPECIALIST'S LEADERSHIP ROLE

The librarians in this project are indispensable members of the team. Working with the teachers, they develop the book lists and review databases. They create the graphic organizers the students use and work individually with them to help them develop essential questions, create final thesis statements, and find statistical and historical research to support their arguments.

CONTRIBUTION TO STUDENT ACHIEVEMENT

This project helps students become better thinkers, researchers, and writers.

FUNDING

This project has been developed over a number of years. It would be impossible to place an actual dollar figure on it, because it has been worked on (mostly during the regular school day) by so many people. The school did fund an instructional growth grant in summer 2005 for three teachers and a librarian to revise and revamp the books lists. This amounted to about $2,000.

EVALUATION

Both teachers and students evaluate this project. The teachers grade the papers, and the students comment on it on the Blackboard site. The team of teachers and librarians assesses the entire project at the end of the year and determines any changes needed for the following year.

Collaboration Districtwide

SUSIE ALEXANDER, LIZ DESKINS, TERRY LORD, MARSHA PFAHL, CHRISTINA H. DORR
HILLIARD CITY SCHOOL DISTRICT, HILLIARD, OHIO

SUMMARY

Collaboration is a hallmark of the Hilliard City School District's library and media program (LMP). To foster the integration of this program into the curriculum, collaborative planning among the library media specialists (LMSs), classroom teachers, technology teachers, and literacy coaches has become a seamless process in the schools' learning environments. The planning process with the teachers varies in every building, depending on the structure of the day and the needs of the students and teachers. With the implementation of Wiggins and McTighe's *Understanding by Design* (UbD) framework, these planning sessions have become increasingly important, even vital, as the team designs quality units of study.[8] These units include learning activities that meet the diversity of learners—their learning styles, interests, and cognitive abilities. Resources are required in multiple formats and readability because the focus of these units is to develop enduring understanding by constructing knowledge through essential questions.

Information literacy skills are critical to the learners. Implementing these units often requires information skills instruction, teaching Eisenberg and Berkowitz's Big6 research process, and the integration of a variety of technology resources.[9] Another powerful benefit of this collaborative planning and teaching method is the reduced ratio of teacher to students that often occurs. The classroom teachers, the LMSs, the technology teachers, and the literacy coaches become a powerful instructional team designing quality work for increasing student achievement.

OBJECTIVES

The main objective of collaboration is to design units and lessons that allow students to build on their strengths and stretch their understandings of curricular skills, processes, and content. To that end, collaboration is a means of combining time, talent, and skills to best design and deliver instruction to all students. Collaboration is an integral part of the two district goals.

The first goal is to implement strategies to improve students' literacy achievement in grades pre-K–12. To accomplish this goal, the LMSs are members of various academic support teams in the buildings, work closely with building literacy coaches and teacher leaders to design instruction and select appropriate literacy resources, and work with students individually and in small groups to scaffold their learning in the reading-writing process. They attend professional development literacy workshops and booktalks, often with collaborating teachers; conduct workshops on informational and media literacy; and create enticing literacy environments in library media centers (LMCs) to meet the needs of students, parents, and teachers,

The second district goal is to develop a deeper knowledge and application of *Understanding by Design* and its role in designing quality work and differentiation with all certified and administrative staff.[10] The LMSs have been designated as the leaders for facilitating the UbD framework in the buildings through thoughtful collaborative planning. They provide support and encouragement as they meet with teams of teachers to develop units and lessons around UbD.

SCHOOL LIBRARY MEDIA SPECIALIST'S LEADERSHIP ROLE

It is fortunate that at Hilliard City School District, the LMS is a curriculum leader in the building. Many times we are the point person in a building and are the first to be trained in new initiatives with the expectation that we will in turn teach and enlighten our staff. This also strengthens our collaborative role; a teacher who is using new curriculum or even new software finds it helpful to have another person who has some experience and will share the load. This gives us an edge, because teachers often want to collaborate with someone who is knowledgeable.

Collaboration works because the LMSs take planning seriously. Although planning to collaborate takes different forms in different buildings, all LMSs realize that careful planning ensures that educational objects are met. Our hope is to have everyone involved with the unit of study and activity meet together. This may mean an English Language Learners teacher, a special education teacher, a literacy coach, or a technology teacher, as well as a grade-level group of teachers, get together initially to talk about curriculum: what needs to be done, the introduction of pertinent materials, or a discussion of what standards need to be met for this unit. UbD assists us in staying focused on the curriculum at hand. After deciding on the standards and what objectives need to be met, we move on to how students will be assessed and what activities will help them reach the objectives, Throughout this discussion, the LMS is usually taking notes, asking clarifying questions, and making suggestions to be sure students' learning styles and developmental needs are being considered.

Implementing the unit requires collaboration. Schedules need to be synchronized and time allotted to discuss revisions throughout the teaching of the unit. Flexibility is key. The LMSs need to be sure all library materials—computers, software, or other technology needs—are ready, and if other print resources are needed, they must be sure these are ordered in a timely manner.

Collaboration takes many steps, lots of time, and, first and foremost, trust. Trust is the most difficult part; it means working with someone else and having that person trust you enough to hand over a portion of instruction. Building trust takes time and may happen gradually. Sometimes it starts with collecting the necessary materials so that the teacher recognizes the LMS knows what she needs. Sometimes it is team teaching, with the LMS in a strictly supporting role, and finally it can be library media specialist and classroom teacher working equally, with the final outcome being increased student achievement. One of the most exciting parts of implementation is devising ways to best meet the learning needs of students, and with the LMS in a teaching role, this can sometimes lead to small group or one-on-one instruction for the student.

In a perfect world, at the end of every unit the parties involved formally evaluate the collaborative unit, deciding what to keep, what to revise, and what to discard. In the real world, this is much more difficult to do. Sometimes the evaluation take place over lunch or even a few minutes in the hallway. In the UbD framework, reflection is an important piece, and we strongly encourage our original team to come back together to discuss and evaluate the unit. Again, the LMS often takes notes to provide a record of the unit for the next time the unit is taught.

Depending on the age of the students, it is also beneficial to get student input. Valuable information can be learned from asking those most directly affected: the students. From creating a formal survey to an informal group discussion, students can be included to assess the success of a particular activity and to elicit ideas for broadening or narrowing a project. The LMS can be instrumental in creating this survey or facilitating the discussion so that the classroom teacher can sit back and observer her students' reactions.

CONTRIBUTIONS TO STUDENT ACHIEVEMENT

Collaborative planning by LMSs, classroom teachers, and other support staff means that more educators are sharing the job of supporting and ultimately increasing student achievement. Collaboration among education professionals that includes a certified library media specialist ensures that all available resources to support students' learning will be considered; curriculum will be integrated across subject areas; and lifelong literacies, such as information and visual, economic, scientific, and technological literacies, will be infused into student learning and achievement. Thoughtful collaboration "pools expertise about curriculum, resources, how students learn, and assessments of individual students."[11]

Achievement is increased as students become skillful users and producers of information by investigating emerging questions, brainstorming resources, locating and using information, synthesizing information into new formats, and evaluating their problem-solving process and the final product. Collaborative planning and teaching ensure that students will work alongside a variety of professionals who can address each student's unique needs, challenges, and celebrations.

As collaborative planning teams that include LMSs come together to design quality work for students, LMCs become central to the implementation and success of that work. LMCs evolve into busy, purposeful learning environments alive with learning communities: "webs of individuals (students, teachers, administrators) who are interconnected in a lifelong quest for understanding. Effective collaboration helps to create a vibrant and engaged community of learners which in turn increases student achievement and success in today's world."[12]

CONCLUSION

Collaboration districtwide is an initiative that requires board of education and central office expectations and support—both human and material resources. It also takes a building administrator that sees the value of several teachers planning collectively rather than in isolation. The LMP schedule needs to be designed to allow time for planning, implementing, and evaluating units of study. But ultimately it is the library media specialist in every building who furthers the process. Each LMS at Hilliard implements collaboration a bit differently, but each takes her charge very seriously.

Collaborative Planning and Curriculum Development for Library Media Specialists and Teachers

PATRICIA PICKARD
DEKALB COUNTY SCHOOL SYSTEM, DECATUR, GEORGIA

SUMMARY

Sixteen state studies regarding the impact of the library media program on student achievement continue to emphasize the importance of collaboration between library media specialists (LMSs) and teachers. Collaborative planning and curriculum development occur in schools and centers of the DeKalb County School System to varying degrees and levels of frequencies. Many of the collaborative relationships have developed over time, while others are just beginning to bloom. Following are best practices used in schools and at the school system level to promote collaboration between LMSs and teachers:

Professional learning classes designed to promote collaboration have been conducted for LMSs and for teams of teachers and LMSs. Discussing the components of the collaborative process and successful collaborations conducted in local schools sets the stage for increasing the number and importance of collaboration.

A variety of locally developed forms are available for use by LMSs in collaborative planning sessions (exhibit 2.1). Each captures information about the components of the assignment and strengthens the communication between the LMS and teachers. Capitalizing on the availability and use of computer technology in schools, many forms have hyperlinks to state and national subject content standards and American Association of School Librarians information literacy standards to ease the design of instructional activities. Using FirstClass, the school system's internal e-mail and conferencing system, reduces the lag time in communications between LMSs and teachers about class instruction and assignments and increases the number of communication exchanges about instructional activities and scheduling classes into the library media center (LMC).

Communication between LMSs and public librarians about students' research assignments is critical when ensuring availability of resources and assistance from the public library staff. Contacts are made between school and public library professionals by telephone calls, faxes, or the electronic school assignment alert form, which includes key components of the assignment to help to direct the kind of assistance and types of resources students need.

OBJECTIVES

There is a growing emphasis by administrators in the curriculum division of the school system to expand collaborative partnerships among educators. This corporate effort to improve collaboration gives greater emphasis to collaboration between LMSs and teachers. Two objectives are being targeted in relation to collaboration:

➤ supporting the systemwide mandate related to vertical and horizontal collaboration
➤ demonstrating how collaborative instructional activities planned by the LMSs and teachers improve student achievement and foster lifelong learning

SCHOOL LIBRARY MEDIA SPECIALIST'S LEADERSHIP ROLE

In many schools, LMSs serve on the school leadership team. This forum provides them opportunities to share how the library media program aligns with the school's mission of improving student

---

Henderson Middle School Collaborative Planning Guide

Subject _____   Grade/Team _____   Library Media Specialists: Ms. Evett/Ms. Heller   Teacher(s) _____

Topic or thematic unit: _____

Planning (1) _____ (2) _____ (3) _____   Instruction Date(s) (1) _____ (2) _____ (3) _____

Instruction Time(s) (1) _____ (2) _____ (3) _____

General Goals	Lesson Objectives	Prior Information Skills Required	Information Skills Needed	Instruction	Materials	Evaluation	Comments

DeKalb County (GA) School System

EXHIBIT 2.1   LOCALLY DEVELOPED COLLABORATIVE PLANNING GUIDE

achievement. Membership on the leadership committee opens avenues for LMSs to introduce or reinforce the benefits of collaboration as new instructional initiatives are proposed at their school. Evaluation of this leadership role is ongoing, but formal and informal comments by school administrators, teachers, and LMSs to administrators of the systemwide library media program indicate meaningful changes are being made and influencing the instructional program.

CONTRIBUTIONS TO STUDENT ACHIEVEMENT

Formalizing the collaboration process between LMSs and teachers has been an evolutionary process. Beginning as short notes in a "grade book," the forms for recording collaborative planning of instructional activities now reflect alignment with state curriculum standards and information literacy standards and skills, as well as recommended resources, an evaluation rubric, and the division of instructional responsibilities for the LMS and teacher (exhibit 2.2). This documentation

Guide for Collaborative Planning

Grade/Team _____ Subject(s) _____ Topic or Thematic Unit _____

Library Media Specialist(s) _____ Teacher(s) _____

Today's Date _____ Instructional Date(s) _____ Time(s) _____

Information Literacy Checklist* Information Literary Standards for Student Learning*	GA Performance Standards*	CRCT Objectives* High School Graduation Tests*	Teacher(s) Responsibilities	Library Media Specialist(s) Responsibilities	Materials/ Resources/ Technology	Evaluation	Comments

*Hyperlinks connect to websites in these areas.

Suggested by Juanita W. Buddy
DeKalb County (GA) School System

EXHIBIT 2.2   FORM FOR REPORTING COLLABORATIVE PLANNING

is also valuable to the LMS as a collection development tool for weeding outdated materials and purchasing new resources that support instructional units. The collaboration process creates a spirit of support and advocacy among teachers for the library media program. All of these benefits of collaboration have an impact on student achievement.

FUNDING

Collaborative planning generally occurs during the school day, and additional funds generally are not needed. Any special collaborative and curriculum planning sponsored by the principal outside the school day is paid for by the principal through funds from the Department of Professional Learning of the school system or through external funding, such as Title I.

EVALUATION

Evaluation of the collaborative process and its benefits is conducted and maintained by the LMSs in the schools. Administrators of the systemwide library media program learn about collaboratively planned activities in schools by reading minutes from school library media and technology meetings, which may include references to successful collaborations, visiting schools and observing classes engaging in collaboratively planned activities, and learning about quality collaborative efforts during professional learning classes.

Constructing a Keyword Search

KATHERINE LOWE
BOSTON ARTS ACADEMY/FENWAY HIGH SCHOOL LIBRARY AND BOSTON SYMPHONY
ORCHESTRA EDUCATION RESOURCE CENTER, BOSTON, MASSACHUSETTS

Teachers of grade 11 students in humanities classes at Fenway High School were concerned that although students may be self-proclaimed experts at searching the Web, they in fact did not know how to construct an effective online search. Many students simply typed an entire question into the search field and gave up if this method did not yield satisfactory results. The teachers admitted that they themselves felt ill equipped to teach their students this skill, so I developed a grid that students could use to identify keywords before they began looking for information online and demonstrated its use for the teachers with one of their humanities classes.

First, the students and I filled out a keyword grid for the topic of hurricanes (prevalent in the news at the time), brainstorming related terms and synonyms, as well as broader and narrower terms (exhibit 2.3). I showed them how to use the thesaurus in Microsoft Word to find keywords when they had exhausted their own knowledge of a topic.

Next, we moved on to their assigned topics: Maslow's hierarchy of needs, Freud's psychoanalytic theory, and the Oedipus complex. Since students had little previous knowledge of these subjects and could come up with only a few keywords on their own, I showed them how to use the library's

Research Topic or Question:

_____

_____

_____

_____

_____

WHO WHAT WHEN WHERE HOW WHY

Keyword(s)/Phrase(s)	Related Words or Synonyms	Broader	Narrower

EXHIBIT 2.3 IDENTIFYING KEYWORDS, RELATED TERMS, SYNONYMS, AND KEY PHRASES

online catalog to find more keywords, particularly related and broader terms, in the notes and subject headings fields of the material records. I also provided them with short articles from World Book Online and guided them through highlighting more keywords. Finally, I gave the students a one-page handout that would remind them of the steps we used in class when they searched on their own in the library the following day.

One of the humanities teachers developed a worksheet for the students to fill out when they researched their topics in the library. Students were required to find at least one print source by searching the online catalog and to use the subscription databases on our library web page (http://fenway.boston.k12.ma.us/library/) to find articles from an online encyclopedia and SIRS Knowledge Source. On the worksheet, they recorded their topic, what they already knew about it, what they needed to learn, keywords used, and citation information for each source found. After her class's library visit, one teacher reported, "I informally asked the class about their results. They agreed that their research was easier to do, and they got better information than if they had done it their own way. A little success!"

The Georgia Helen Ruffin Reading Bowl

PATRICIA PICKARD
DEKALB COUNTY SCHOOL SYSTEM, DECATUR, GEORGIA

SUMMARY

Several years ago, Helen Ruffin was the dynamic library media specialist (LMS) at Sky Haven Elementary School in DeKalb County, Georgia. In 1985, she served on the selection committee for the Georgia Children's Book Award nominee program. This literature program, which began in the Department of Language Education at the University of Georgia's College of Education, inspired her to use the nominated books to encourage her students to read.

Ruffin created a unique reading competition, the Reading Bowl, in game format using the award nominees. Her vision was to have teams comprising students from different schools compete to test their knowledge of the selected books. She shared this vision with her colleagues, who embraced her idea and pressed forward. This group, which became the grassroots steering committee, opened its arms to other interested members.

The DeKalb County Helen Ruffin Reading Bowl (HRRB) Steering Committee still directs all components of the HRRB. The first system bowl was held in 2000, with only elementary participants. Today the bowl is open to students in grades 4 through 12. High schools joined the reading bowl in 2002, using the Georgia Peach Teen Readers Choice Award nominees, established that year for this function.

Realizing the impact the bowl was having on participants and schools, the steering committee decided to spread the word throughout the state. As a result of the committee's efforts, the first statewide competition was held in 2003. The Georgia Children's Book Award program became partner to the Georgia HRRB. The bowl grew so large that the committee added regional bowls to the configuration. With the help of the Georgia Association of Educators and the Georgia Library Media Association, the Georgia Helen Ruffin Reading Bowl sponsored the Northern Regional and the Southern Regional competitions on the same day, March 19, 2005. The winning teams met at the Georgia Children's Literature Conference in Athens, Georgia, on April 30, 2005, for the state championship of the Georgia HRRB.

In an effort to spread the word even more, six members of the Georgia Steering Committee participated in the American Association of School Librarians' Exploratorium on October 6, 2005, in Pittsburgh. "Get on Board with the Helen Ruffin Reading Bowl" was a stopping point for attendees. Participants had the opportunity to talk with Georgia Steering Committee members, watch a looping PowerPoint presentation, collect handouts, and try their hand with the buzzer in a sample round. From all indications, the committee's message, "The reading bowl is a unique way to use your state's book award nominees to increase appreciation of literature, reading comprehension and test scores," was well received. (Information on the HRRB can be found at http://www.dekalb .k12.ga.us/hrrb/.)

OBJECTIVES

The qualitative and quantitative objectives of the HRRB state that students will

- ➤ increase standardized test scores
- ➤ improve academic achievement
- ➤ increase reading comprehension
- ➤ develop an appreciation for literature
- ➤ enhance verbal communication skills
- ➤ promote cooperation
- ➤ build self-esteem
- ➤ develop team spirit

The HRRB program models an effective use of books as sources of pleasure and information. It encourages the use of both school library and public library resources in making the book award nominees available for all students. The group discussion about the books after each student has read a reading bowl book promotes higher student achievement. These discussions also promote increased vocabulary and assist students in becoming information literate, objectives that are aligned with the system's goal of improving students' reading proficiency and information literacy skills in all schools. There is tremendous enthusiasm in support of the reading bowl in the system because participation enables students of various socioeconomic backgrounds to compete on an even footing in a group setting.

Reading is the key and the equalizer. Research shows that reading proficiency increases with practice. Students participating in this competition have shown marked increases in their standardized test scores. For example, a sample population of HRRB participants showed an average increase of forty points in reading over two years.

SCHOOL LIBRARY MEDIA SPECIALIST'S LEADERSHIP ROLE

The dedicated steering committee, composed of LMSs, plans and implements all components of the bowl. The work of the committee includes advertising and publicity; sponsorships; team and corporate banners; T-shirt design competition; registration; program; training of moderators, scorekeepers, and console judges; and trophies and certificates.

CONTRIBUTIONS TO STUDENT ACHIEVEMENT

Student achievement has been measured in a sample population as described above. The involvement of LMSs in the bowl extends the library program outside the media center. Many teams have a classroom teacher and an LMS as co-coaches. This collaboration improves the working relationship of the pair. Some of the participating LMSs have commented to steering committee members that students, teachers, and staff realize the value of the library program and the impact of the reading bowl on student learning and achievement.

FUNDING

Participating teams pay $35 to register for the HRRB competition. In addition, the committee seeks donations from sponsors.

EVALUATION

This best practice is evaluated each year in terms of participation, attendance, and impact on student learning and achievement. The HRRB began as a county competition in 2000 with sixteen teams. In 2005, there were forty-one elementary, fourteen middle, and five high schools. In 2006, forty-four elementary, eighteen middle, and eight high schools registered. Each year evaluation forms are given to coaches and volunteers, and the following changes have been made as a result of feedback received on the evaluation forms:

- ➤ Alternative titles have been eliminated.
- ➤ Scoring has become more accurate with the introduction of electronic scoring, which is used in conjunction with paper forms.
- ➤ Each team is introduced during a parade of banners depicting each school team. This has made the bowl more interactive, limiting the opening assembly to a short introduction of all platform guests and reading of the rules.

In Harmony: A Collaborative Workshop for Librarian/Music Teacher Pairs

KATHERINE LOWE
BOSTON ARTS ACADEMY/FENWAY HIGH SCHOOL LIBRARY AND BOSTON SYMPHONY ORCHESTRA EDUCATION RESOURCE CENTER, BOSTON, MASSACHUSETTS

School librarians and their music teacher colleagues attended a full-day in-service workshop that I planned and facilitated with a member of my school's music faculty. We modeled teacher/librarian collaboration by role-playing how we selected resources, co-planned, and taught together to embed information literacy skills into the music collaboration. Participants had an opportunity to preview materials in our Education Resource Center (ERC) and brainstorm ideas for projects they could implement in their own schools. The resource center contains over $100,000 worth of equipment and materials purchased over five years with funds from a federal education grant obtained by the Boston Symphony Orchestra's (BSO) Office of Education and Community Programs to support the teaching of the arts in Massachusetts. Each school year, the BSO provides a series of arts-related professional development workshops for K–12 teachers in our ERC.

Together librarians and music teachers attending the In Harmony workshop discovered the differences among cooperating, coordinating, and collaborating to ensure student success and boost achievement. Participants experience a sequencing activity that demonstrates the best point at which to include the school librarian in the planning process: the very beginning! Teams were provided with research paper alternatives and given an opportunity to brainstorm project ideas with their partners before sharing them with the group. All participants completed an evaluation of the workshop and returned to their schools to plan and implement a project with their partner.[13]

In order to receive professional development points, each pair was required to plan, implement, and evaluate a project at their school and share it by e-mail with the other participants. Along with a written description of their project, each pair completed a Class Visit Planning Form and a Collaborative Unit Evaluation Form.[14]

The workshop was jointly funded by the BSO and the Massachusetts School Library Media Association (MSLMA). MSLMA, as the state's professional organization for school librarians, provided the participants with professional development points required for continued teacher certification. BSO and MSLMA shared the cost of $150 stipends for each of the presenters and $500 for a light breakfast and lunch for the workshop participants.

Junior Theme and Immigration Thesis

MARILYN COBB
NEW TRIER HIGH SCHOOL—WINNETKA CAMPUS, WINNETKA, ILLINOIS

SUMMARY

The Immigration Thesis Theme for members of the junior class occurs over a three-month period, from making title choices to writing the final seven- to ten-page paper. The decision to move from an author paper with an emphasis on literary criticism to an immigration theme was the result of discussions between the lead teacher and librarian. The goal was to find a method that would more fully engage the students in the writing and research process and broaden their literary horizons by exposing them to a larger variety of literature.

The suggested list of books is divided into the following broad categories: European, Middle Easter, Hispanic, Asian, and Other. Then a subcategory is created for specific ethnic groups. In many cases, the students choose books that relate to their own ethnicity. They must read two books and make weekly entries on Blackboard discussing their reactions to the books and their writing and research experience. Because the teacher and the librarian read the entries, they have a common understanding of how all the students are doing throughout the entire process.

When the initial reading is completed, the students begin a four-week period in the library where they research their authors, formulate a thesis statement, and study the particular immigrant experience. The librarian introduces an online pathfinder that includes relevant databases, reference materials, and websites. The librarian emphasizes the research process, and the teacher focuses on the mechanics and content of the paper.

OBJECTIVE

The main objective of the junior theme is to learn a process for doing research and composition that results in a well-documented paper based on a logically presented argument.

SCHOOL LIBRARY MEDIA SPECIALIST'S LEADERSHIP ROLE

The librarian and teacher work closely to develop the original book list and essential question. The essential question guides the plan of action the student will follow in completing the research needed to support their argument. During the time in the library, the librarian works with the whole class and individual students to teach, find, and evaluate sources.

CONTRIBUTION TO STUDENT ACHIEVEMENT

The project helps students become better researchers and writers.

FUNDING

The project is part of the normal school year and does not receive any special funding.

EVALUATION

The project has several internal deadlines that are graded along with the final overall grade for the completed paper. There is a detailed rubric for the student's use to make sure all requirements are met. The English teachers and librarians informally evaluate the project each year.

Junior Theme with Special Education Students
ANGELA BURNS
NEW TRIER HIGH SCHOOL—WINNETKA CAMPUS, WINNETKA, ILLINOIS

SUMMARY

Junior Theme is a semester project that all junior-level English classes must complete before moving on to senior level. The Special Education Junior Theme is often a modified version of what the regular classes accomplish. The success of this project is a result of the collaboration between the special education teacher and the librarian working with the special education class. Students choose a topic, usually a current issue, and begin their research with an idea of where they stand and what their opinion is on it. Students in a regular junior-level class are given a list of required sources and goals before beginning the assignment.

For special education classes, modifications are made to the assignment, although the goals and finished product are the same: a complete, well-thought-out paper. Students need to have at least two book sources; two magazine or newspaper sources, which can come from a periodical database; and one reference source (encyclopedia or reference database). They also have to keep a folder, organized by subtopics, in which they store their note cards, outline, and graphic organizer.

Because this is a collaborative assignment, the teacher and librarian present the information as a team. The teacher often starts by presenting the students with a packet that clearly states the goals for each day and then each week. The teacher and the librarian then explain the function of the folder and how to organize it by subtopic. The librarian teaches the students how to use a graphic organizer to draw together ideas for each subtopic. This graphic organizer is essential to the student's success because it includes an essential question, devised by the teacher, that is general for all topics, and the answer to this question can serve as the thesis to the paper. The librarian also helps students choose books, provides a lesson on how to search databases, and helps with selecting ideas for subtopics. As students continue to research, they often need extra help with ideas for the note cards, with how to do bibliographical citations, and with organizing their paper. The librarian and teacher work closely with individual students to help them to complete their paper.

OBJECTIVES

The major objective of this project is to help students with learning disabilities synthesize information in a clear and concise way that they can understand, create a well-written paper, and feel proud of putting it all together. The goal is to give all special education students the same learning opportunities as students in regular education classes. Modifying the project for the various special needs shows that all students can achieve.

SCHOOL LIBRARY MEDIA SPECIALIST'S LEADERSHIP ROLE

The librarian is a major contributor to this project. She worked with the special education teacher to modify the original junior theme, helped in selecting the topics, reviewed databases for possible research sources, and worked on the bibliographical information. The major contribution was the graphic organizer students used to develop their subtopics and thesis.

CONTRIBUTION TO STUDENT ACHIEVEMENT

This project helps students who are generally labeled as incapable achieve confidence in their abilities to synthesize information and become better learners and researchers.

FUNDING

This project was created during the school day, mainly during common prep periods, between teacher and librarian. It was developed as part of the regular job, which is to develop curriculum and collaborate on projects.

EVALUATION

The project is evaluated mainly by the special education teacher, who grades the papers, checks for the student's understanding, and collects all the pieces: the folder, note cards, outline, and graphic organizer. Part of the evaluation is done during collaboration with the librarian because the project extends over several weeks.

Kapolei High School Library Media Center Teaching and Learning

CAROLYN KIRIO
KAPOLEI HIGH SCHOOL LIBRARY MEDIA CENTER, KAPOLEI, HAWAII

SUMMARY

Kapolei High School's library media program is fully integrated into the school curriculum. At Kapolei, ninth- and tenth-grade students are members of integrated teams containing the same core teachers for English, science, and social studies. In eleventh and twelfth grades, they select enrollment from among nine career pathway academies. Their work and senior projects are focused on investigating aspects of their personal interest, chosen career, or academic discipline. With collaborative teaming and services provided through curriculum leadership, the library staff infuses information literacy standards within each unit and lesson plan design. Information literacy skills are incorporated into projects and activities so students learn to become proactive and effective users of information.

OBJECTIVES

The high school librarians have worked with the individual academies within the Kapolei High School complex to establish an information skills curriculum that is scaffolded K–12. Librarians at the high school use this scope and sequence to build on students' prior knowledge and tailor instruction to develop skills needed for lifelong learning. Kapolei High librarians meet quarterly with their complex area feeder schools (four elementary schools, one middle school, and one high school). With their prospective students' library media specialists, they facilitate the discussion on improving information literacy instruction, curriculum, and assessment. Collaboratively they create innovative, effective library lessons and units to promote increased student achievement pre-kindergarten to twelfth grade.

The library staff serve as active members of the school's curriculum support cadre. Through collaborative teaming with teachers and academies, librarians create and assist in the implementation of project-based units and lessons. To provide guidance to different disciplines, they have blended subjects into cohesive units and integrative project-based learning activities. Teachers partner with library media specialists to enrich their classes with research skills and various information resources.

The librarians participate in different degrees of collaboration. For many teams, the library is brought in from the beginning. Serving as a member of the team, the librarian helps to develop an idea or concept into a rigorous, integrated, project-based learning unit. For other teachers, librarians' participation may be limited to introducing resources and presenting information literacy skills. Ultimately for many projects, the librarians participate in team teaching and the assessment of student projects and presentations. Through this active involvement, librarians collect and analyze data to determine the effectiveness of their information literacy lessons and, based on their conclusions,

School Library Media Program Assessment

PREPARED BY THE AMERICAN ASSOCIATION OF SCHOOL LIBRARIANS TEACHING FOR LEARNING TASK FORCE SUBCOMMITTEE

Please check (✓) one that applies for each Target Indicator. Leave blank if you are not yet at the basic level. Write notes in the comments section to use in setting goals.

A. Teaching and Learning

Target Indicators	Basic	Proficient	Exemplary	Comments
1. Information Literacy Standards are integrated into content learning.	❏ Students learn to use library materials in the context of classroom content. Library skills are locational skills or how to find information.	❏ The library media program provides essential support to the curriculum. Students learn information literacy skills, which extend beyond location to analysis, evaluation, and use of information through collaborative efforts of teachers and the library media specialist.	❏ The library media program is a catalyst for intellectual inquiry. Students learn to incorporate information literacy skills into their work and become proactive users of information and resources.	
2. Collaborative planning is modeled and promoted.	❏ Discussions take place between the library media specialist and teacher regarding lessons and the curriculum.	❏ Some teachers and the library media specialist collaboratively plan and teach curriculum units.	❏ The school schedule ensures time for the teachers and the library media specialist to regularly meet at common planning times to plan instructional units, learning strategies, and activities. The library media specialist helps build a coordinated instructional program.	
3. Curriculum development is modeled and promoted.	❏ The library media program reflects the curriculum and curriculum guides and/or information is provided to teachers and the library media specialist.	❏ School policies enable the library media specialist to participate in building and districtwide curriculum meetings and share knowledge and resources.	❏ The district encourages the library media specialist to work collaboratively with administrators and teachers in planning, developing, and writing curriculum.	
4. Effective teaching is modeled and promoted.	❏ The library media specialist participates in directing activities and assessment of student work.	❏ Teaching is generally facilitative. The teacher and/or library media specialist may prescribe the strategies, research questions, or assessment products to be used.	❏ Teaching is facilitative, collaborative, and creative. Reflection and authentic assessment are built into all instructional units.	

Source: From *A Planning Guide for Information Power: Building Partnerships for Learning with School Library Media Program Assessment Rubric for the Twenty-first Century* (Chicago: ALA and AASL, 1999), 35.

EXHIBIT 2.4   RUBRIC TO ASSESS THE LIBRARY PROGRAM

work to improve student achievement results. Through data-driven dialogue, the librarians can track student progress and make adjustments to the overall curriculum.

In an effort to foster individual and collaborative inquiry, Kapolei librarians have developed and implemented the senior project experience. Designed to be an exhibit of mastery of standards, students showcase their knowledge and application of research skills through the creation, development, implementation, and presentation of an in-depth research project based on possible career choices or other interests. Students conduct all phases of the research process, from identifying an essential question to developing an original product or idea. The process and products are then documented in a portfolio, presented, and assessed by a panel of community experts. To help students prepare for this monumental research undertaking, elements of individual inquiry are introduced at earlier grade levels through project-based learning units and projects.

SCHOOL LIBRARY MEDIA SPECIALIST'S LEADERSHIP ROLE

In addition to collaborating and reflecting with teachers and subject-area teams, the librarians serve as curriculum instructional leaders. Working with different grade levels, Sandy Yamamoto and I, both librarians, assist the assistant principals in identifying areas of need and executing teaching/learning workshops for our professional learning communities. We meet regularly to plan teaching concepts and strategies that support curriculum and instruction and to develop a plan of action for training teachers.

EVALUATION

The library media specialists conduct program analysis and long-range planning, which is reflected in the library's five-year action plan. Data are collected through diagnostic, summative, and formative methods. Yearly goals are developed based on student and curriculum needs. Elements identified help plan for budget and the acquisition of instructional materials. At the end of the school year, an in-depth analysis is conducted based on rubrics created to assess the school library program (exhibit 2.4).[15] The information gained from the study results help to adjust long-range plans and motivate the librarians and administration to improve and refine school programs, curriculum development, and academic services.

Librarian + Teacher:
Designing Powerful Learning Activities

JULIE HYDE-PORTER
CHERRY CREEK HIGH SCHOOL, GREENWOOD VILLAGE, COLORADO

SUMMARY

Teacher and librarian collaboration is naturally fostered by an Adventure of the American Mind–Colorado (AAM-CO), a program funded by the Library of Congress. The goal of this program, which has affiliates in other states, is to help teachers design learning activities that enhance the quality of education through the use of technology and the immense digitized collections available online at the Library of Congress website (http://www.loc.gov).

To initiate involvement in this program, I attended a series of three AAM-CO workshops to learn methods for finding, accessing, using, and teaching with primary sources. The first workshop was invaluable in gaining an understanding of the vast and somewhat confusing organization of the Library of Congress site. Learning how to browse and navigate the collections and practice with a variety of search strategies made accessing specific information more expedient. It was beneficial to browse the teacher-created lesson plans and learn instructional strategies for incorporating primary sources into classroom lessons.

The second workshop focused on analyzing the various formats of primary sources: photographs, films, cartoons, documents, interviews, and music. I learned techniques for engaging students to think critically about these sources and ways to make history real and relevant for them.

The third workshop taught me techniques for creating activities and presentations using PowerPoint, Dreamweaver, and other technology applications.

After completing these workshops, I was eligible to participate in the AAM-CO 2005 Summer Learning Activities Development Project. I asked two Cherry Creek High School social studies teachers if they were interested in submitting a proposal to collaboratively plan a learning activity using primary sources. They were enthusiastic about this opportunity and agreed to participate if I helped them access the primary source for the Library of Congress and teach them what I had learned in the workshops. Our proposal, Immigration to the United States, was tailored for ninth-grade American history classes with modifications for use in world history classes and other disciplines.

After our proposal was accepted by the project, we attended several professional development days at Metropolitan State College, home of the Adventure of the American Mind–Colorado. Experts in the field of instructional design presented ideas for incorporating primary sources into the curriculum, best teaching practices, and lesson alignment with state standards. We were given time, materials, templates, and compensation for developing learning activities. The content expertise of the social studies teachers helped to solidify the essential research questions and provided background knowledge necessary to design lessons that aligned with subject-area curriculum. My librarian's understanding of how to access quality information and integrate the use of appropriate technologies ensured that all steps of the research process were embedded in the lesson design.

We designed our learning activity using templates provided for teacher instruction and student lessons. Our learning activity, "The Immigrant Experience in the United States: 1850–1930; A KnowledgeQuest for High School Social Studies Students," complete with resources, learning standards, student tasks, sample worksheets, and rubrics, is available at the project website: http://aamcolorado.mscd.edu/learnactComp.htm.

OBJECTIVES

The objectives of this project were focused on improving the research and critical thinking skills of Cherry Creek students to prepare them for college. This objective was supported by librarians and teachers collaboratively planning and creating meaningful learning activities in support of multiple learning standards in history:

- ➤ increase students' understanding of the process and resources of historical inquiry
- ➤ understand that societies are diverse and have changed over time
- ➤ understand the chronological organization of history and know how to organize events and people into major eras to identify and explain historical relationships

In addition, this project supported student attainment of information literacy standards:

- ➤ the ability to access, evaluate, and use information
- ➤ the ability to differentiate between primary and secondary sources
- ➤ the ability to recognize, analyze, and draw inferences from various types of primary sources
- ➤ the ability to engage in learning through analyzing primary sources and using various technologies to create research projects

SCHOOL LIBRARY MEDIA SPECIALIST'S LEADERSHIP ROLE

The librarian was responsible for attending the initial AAM-CO workshops to keep current with best practices for integrating new digitized resources in the curriculum. Because of this training, the school was provided funding to acquire scanners, document projectors, and other equipment for teachers to use in preparing and presenting lessons in their classrooms. The librarian initiated the involvement of social studies teachers in the Learning Activities Development Program, and she also informed other teachers and librarians about the program and encouraged them to attend subsequent training opportunities. Further staff development classes will be offered at school.

CONTRIBUTIONS TO STUDENT ACHIEVEMENT

Because the collaborative relationship between the librarian and the social studies teachers has grown stronger, other teachers have requested assistance in redesigning lessons that introduce primary resources into research projects. In addition, other librarians and teachers are attending the AAM-CO training. Students are more engaged in the research process and are developing more sophisticated critical thinking skills through analyzing and synthesizing primary documents.

FUNDING

Funds for the development of the initial learning activity were provided by a Library of Congress grant that provided $400 per teacher and an additional allocation of $200 of two in-service workshops presented the following year. Teachers could obtain state or university credit at a reduced rate in our district, at their own cost, for attending the series of AAM-CO workshops.

EVALUATION

Student research projects that are part of this curriculum unit will be evaluated based on the criteria

	Beginning (1)	Developing (2)	Accomplished (3)	Exemplary (4)	Score
Understand an immigrant's experience	Takes a position that is inappropriate for the situation. Presents a position that cannot be supported by evidence	Takes a position that the situation does not completely warrant or that is redundant. Does not provide sufficient supporting evidence for the position	Takes a position that is appropriate for the circumstances and supports an underrepresented perspective. Provides sufficient justification for the position	Takes a position that is appropriate for the circumstances and introduces a valuable and unrepresented perspective. Provides strong supporting evidence for the position	1 2 3 4
Written or oral material answers essential questions	Some questions answered but hypotheses unclear	Most questions answered, some hypotheses clear	All questions answered, some hypotheses clear	All questions answered, all hypotheses clear	1 2 3 4
Supporting evidence	Some hypotheses supported by primary sources but link to hypotheses unclear	All hypotheses supported by primary sources but link to hypotheses unclear	All hypotheses supported by primary sources, and link to most hypotheses is clear	All hypotheses supported by primary sources, and all links to hypotheses clear	1 2 3 4
Visual/audio aesthetics	Visual and/or audio portion of presentation is incomplete	Visual and/or audio portion of presentation is complete but presented in an unorganized fashion	Visual and/or audio portion of presentation is complete and well organized	Visual and/or audio portion of presentation is complete, well organized, and includes related elements that go beyond the sources provided or the requirements of the assignment	1 2 3 4
Overall score				_____ / 9 = _____	

Source: "The Immigrant Experience in the United States: 1850–1930; A KnowledgeQuest for High School Social Studies Students." Designed by Julie Hyde-Porter, Kathy McKittrick, and Susan Landers Roberts, page 11. Retrieved February 6, 2008, from http://aamcolorado.mscd.edu/learnactComp.htm.

EXHIBIT 2.5 RUBRIC FOR THE IMMIGRATION LESSON PLAN

established by the classroom teachers' rubrics. A sample rubric is included in the immigration lesson plan (exhibit 2.5). The effectiveness of the library instruction program will be based in part on reviewing statistics on the number of teacher planning meetings and the number of classes incorporating primary sources and its associated technology in their research lessons. And students' and teachers' attitudes toward this project will be determined through a survey.

Middle East Peace Summit

JUDY GRESSEL
NEW TRIER HIGH SCHOOL—NORTHFIELD CAMPUS, NORTHFIELD, ILLINOIS

SUMMARY

Ninth graders investigate history, politics, foreign policy, and international relations related to the Palestinian-Israeli conflict and Iraq War during a nine-week study of the Middle East in World History at New Trier High School. With librarian collaboration, teachers Kerry Hall, Carolyn Muir, and David Hjelmgren developed a monthlong project focusing on the controversial, complex, and current Middle East environment.

Working in pairs, students take the role of a world leader, keep a research journal, develop a friend and foe list, analyze controversial situations in a thoughtful essay, and, as the culminating experience, share their views and debate ideas at a Middle East Peace Summit. The process has the feel of a Model UN exercise in which students grapple with significant issues and try to make sense of complicated information using an array of print and recent electronic resources.

This is a challenging project because ninth graders have no particular knowledge base or special interest in Middle East affairs. Before the library research, teachers familiarize students with the major countries, leaders, groups, movements, and relationships in the region. Because the topic is heavily covered by the media but coverage tends to be superficial and biased, librarians at New Trier have played a key role in resource development. They guide students to a wide variety of first-rate resources and organize those sources so that students understand which sources are pro-Israeli, pro-Arab, or neutral. Students need to interact with delegates from other countries to speak effectively for their nation during the role-play simulation. They need to become fluent with viewpoints held by key countries on a variety of critical issues and be able to answer difficult questions: How can a just and lasting peace be achieved in the Middle East between Israelis and Palestinians? How have events since 1967 affected the possible peace? How might stability come to Iraq? How can Iraq make strides toward democracy? Has the Iraq War helped or hurt the democratization of the Middle East? What are the pros and cons of going to war in Iraq?

For this inquiry-oriented activity, librarians collaborated with teachers six weeks prior to the start of the project, working on essential questions and building a website intentionally designed to make best use of limited student time. Links to biographical information on leaders and actual leader quotes are given in context (http://www.newtrier.k12.il.us/library/teacher_assignments/ MiddleEast/default_northfield.htm).

Citations to the full-text articles are provided so that students can locate articles in periodical databases easily. The focus is on students' use of information and support of students' thinking at the levels of analysis, synthesis, and evaluation. Researching as partners, students can share information and thus achieve a higher degree of preparation for role play. Role play is an important technique in the area of experiential learning; it not only has a motivational aspect but also makes remembering easier long after the project ends.

OBJECTIVES

➤ Students will read widely to understand the complexity of Middle East history and politics.

➤ Students will develop a solid understanding of the position of their role (leader) and his or her adversaries.

➤ Students will learn to infer when assessing world leaders' statements and be able to recognize political bias.

➤ Students will be able to create strong arguments supported by fact.

➤ Students will incorporate oral arguments in a role play of world leader discussions and negotiations and expand their ability to see other points of view.

SCHOOL LIBRARY MEDIA SPECIALIST'S LEADERSHIP ROLE

In collaboration with teachers, librarians developed the Middle East Peace Summit website to help students manage the volume of information and sources. The task of making judicious resource choices that are useful for this project without a base of knowledge would be insurmountable without librarians teaming with teachers. Librarians organized information, made it accessible, created graphic organizers, and worked with students individually to locate information supporting their arguments.

CONTRIBUTIONS TO STUDENT ACHIEVEMENT

This project enables students to find supporting evidence for oral arguments and written essays, create convincing position statements, and strengthen connections between ideas. After completing the project, the students are literate with databases, as well as with the Internet because they have learned to evaluate websites with a careful eye and skepticism.

FUNDING

This project was developed in 2001 and improved over several years with input from three librarians working during the regular school day. No special funding was required. The improvement is fostered by identifying a library media specialist to serve as the key library liaison to the world history teachers.

EVALUATION

The project includes the process of ongoing planning and improvement each year. It is kept up-to-date as significant world issues emerge each year. It is evaluated by both the teachers and students who assess the process and the product. Teachers grade the students' research journals, essays, and oral arguments; peer evaluation and self-evaluation are also included. At least one librarian is present for the peace summit to give feedback to teachers and assess the effectiveness of the research process.

Library and Technology Orientation for New Teachers

SHARON COIL
CHERRY CREEK HIGH SCHOOL, GREENWOOD VILLAGE, COLORADO

SUMMARY

Educating and orienting new teachers to the library is a priority at Cherry Creek High School. Our administration has given us valuable time before school begins with teachers new to our school. This day for building new relationships, offering our services, and inviting teachers to collaborate with teacher-librarians throughout the year requires planning in the spring. As a result we are recognized as instructional leaders and curriculum facilitators, ready to strengthen plans as the year begins.

Each year we change the structure for the day to meet the challenges of the changing program and school; however, several components remain constant:

1. We get to know the new teachers, and they get to learn about us. One year we asked each teacher to consider which book he or she would be and why. Many of them revealed a great deal about their interests and their beliefs in the exchanges. (Later we used these titles in our monthly *Creek Reads* publication.) We participate as well so that teachers get to know us and the importance of reading in our lives and our teaching to encourage and inspire our students.

2. We demonstrate teacher/librarian collaboration: Sometimes one of our veteran teachers will "interrupt" our presentation, pretending to have an urgent need to get her name in the scheduling book. We use her interruption as an opportunity to role-play the scheduling procedures and a typical initial collaborative appointment. In this way, new teachers as well as experienced teachers learn how the library program underscores the school's instructional plans.

3. We clarify the range of our services for students, teachers, and the community. We give each teacher a brochure delineating the details about services we offer, as well as the hours, phone numbers, and personnel. (See http://www.cchs.ccsd.k12.co.us/academics/ dept/lib/about_lib.html.)

4. The heart of our work is modeling the lessons we have created with teachers. We proudly show our teachers' research assignments, which reflect independent, higher-level thinking that will inevitably contribute importantly to student achievement.

5. We explore technology as it relates to library instruction. We teach the use of the school website and within it our library links containing the online catalog, lessons, projects, writing assistance, and much more.

6. We have fun exploring the online catalog and the subscription databases with the new teachers as they begin to discover the valuable resources in our school. Pairing a teacher with someone from a different academic area, we ask them to create a cross-disciplinary collaborative lesson requiring books and database research. They begin with an essential question that spans both disciplines and search for materials in the library and online to share with the others.

7. We involve the teachers. They leave with books for their semester's work, library cards, lesson ideas, and knowledge of our library and the teacher-librarians. At the close of the event, we take their pictures to put in offices as a reminder of who each teacher is as we make plans to work with them soon.

OBJECTIVES

The goal of this practice is to mentor new teachers in library use. We support the district's standards of excellence in research that support student achievement. By connecting content standards with information literacy and technology standards for the new teachers, we support our school, district, and state goals and standards. Acquainting our teachers with the teacher-librarians and making them comfortable in using our facility and materials support them in meeting these goals and standards.

SCHOOL LIBRARY MEDIA SPECIALIST'S LEADERSHIP ROLE

The school library media specialists plan and implement the orientation for new teachers. In the spring we evaluate our program against AASL and AECT's *Information Power,* which provides guidance to schools in developing a student-centered library media program. We reject things that have not worked well in the past and create new plans for the following year. We evaluate the use of the library by our teachers as well as their lessons and our continuing collaboration as part of the process. We keep detailed statistics in a database, developed using Microsoft Access software, to evaluate the numbers. These factors are the basis for creating the teacher orientation as the materials and goals for the next year.

The more effective and powerful our training is, the more dramatic the results are in terms of the work we do with teachers. Their training creates an exciting culture among the new teachers of planning unique, authentic lessons with the teacher-librarians. The circle of using resources and then purchasing new materials to use perpetuates an excellent library and library program. As a result, our students have the instruction and the materials they need to succeed.

Much of our planning is accomplished in weekly library meetings. Our administration provides "curriculum pay" or release time to work on special projects, including the orientation for new teachers. We print the materials, including the brochure, at our school's technology center.

EVALUATION

The orientation is evaluated by the teachers themselves as they answer questions about their first year at the school. We also continually evaluate our progress using our statistics and planning our lessons each week.

Power Readers

KATHERINE LOWE
BOSTON ARTS ACADEMY/FENWAY HIGH SCHOOL LIBRARY, BOSTON, MASSACHUSETTS

SUMMARY

I instituted the Power Readers program to get students excited about books and reading. I asked teachers to identify students who love to read and invited them, plus other students I knew to be avid readers, to recommend a book they thought their friends would enjoy (exhibits 2.6 and 2.7). About fifty students responded with their recommendation, which included a paragraph describing the book and a positive published review of the book they had located. I invited teachers and other staff in our building to participate, and many did, including one of the custodians. I bought five copies of each recommended book for the Power Readers display and had staff and students pose for photos with their books.

I created bookplates for each Power Readers book with the name and grade of the person who recommended it. I made posters of each Power Reader, modeled after ALA's "Read @ your library" posters, and featured two each week on a bulletin board in the hallway outside the library door. These posters were eventually added to the Power Readers gallery inside the library. I also created a web page for the Power Readers photos and book recommendations (see http://fenway.boston.k12.ma.us/library/for_students/power_readers.htm).

FUNDING

I requested and received a portion of our building's Title I funds to purchase the Power Readers

---

Power Readers!

The Power Readers program is designed to generate excitement about books and reading among Fenway and BAA students.

Here's how it works:

- Nominate a book you have read that you would like to recommend to other students.

- Write a paragraph about why this book should be purchased for our library.

- Provide a positive review of this book from a magazine or newspaper.

If your recommendation is accepted, we will purchase the book and display it on the Power Readers bookcase in the library, with a label that indicates that YOU recommended the book.

We will also take a picture of you with your book and turn it into a "READ" poster for the hallway outside the library.

To nominate a book, fill out a Power Readers Book Nomination form and return it to the Library.

EXHIBIT 2.6 POWER READERS INVITATION FOR NOMINATIONS

books. Literacy specialists provided $3,000 from funds earmarked for classroom libraries. They saw the value of having these books accessible to all students in the library rather than restricted to individual classroom collections. Labels for bookplates, gold seals for the covers of Power Readers books, color printer ink, and book-processing supplies were purchased for $300 from the library supply budget. From funds donated to the library by a charitable foundation, I bought two semicircular end-of-ranges display bookcases for $800 each. The displays have become a focal point in the library, centrally located at the end of two low bookcases for reference books opposite the circulation desk.

Students flocked to the Power Readers display to see what books their friends had recommended. The program had the desired effect of getting students to talk about books, check out more books, and read for sheer pleasure. Because we had five copies of each title, friends could read the same books at the same time, and teachers could check out a whole set of books for small reading groups in their classes.

A variation of Power Readers that we are currently using is the Featured Readers program. A student may choose books and other materials, like CDs and videos, from the library collection to create their own display. Students who elect to be Featured Readers earn the privilege of selecting a new book to add to the library collection. A sign bearing the student's name and photo is placed on the display and their poster is exhibited outside the library door.

Power Readers Book Nomination

Please complete and return this form to the library.

Your name: _____ Grade: _____

House (Fenway): _____ Major (BAA): _____

I recommend this book for the Power Readers display in the BAA/Fenway Library:

Title: _____

Author: _____

ISBN: _____

I am recommending this book because _____
_____
_____
_____
_____
_____

Please attach a positive review of this book from a magazine or newspaper. You may use the library's online databases to find a review. If you don't know how, ask for help in the library. This is required for your book to be considered for purchase.

EXHIBIT 2.7 POWER READERS BOOK NOMINATION FORM

Professional Learning

PATRICIA PICKARD
DEKALB COUNTY SCHOOL SYSTEM, DECATUR, GEORGIA

SUMMARY

Historically, the Department of Educational Media provides opportunities for professional learning. Participants include library media specialists (LMSs) and support staff, new principals, and teachers. Throughout the year, a variety of one-hour to five-day classes are presented. Traditionally the training sessions occur after school hours or during the summer. Currently, a miniconference format with concurrent sessions is growing in popularity with LMSs and support staff. The following summary outlines professional development offerings coordinated by the staff of the Department of Educational Media:

School LMSs attend sessions focusing on a variety of professional topics, including information literacy standards and the alignment with state curriculum standards, children's and young adult literature, computer technology related to online resources, library automation, media technology associated with digital video, and use and promotion of the statewide virtual library, GALILEO. Special sessions are conducted in conjunction with the technology department of the school system for web page design. New LMSs participate in special classes designed to address library administrative practices and policies unique to the school system.

Library media clerks and secretaries work with LMSs to provide effective library media programs in each school. Classes focus on clerical tasks related to library administration, basic information about ready-reference print and online resources, minor maintenance of audiovisual equipment, library automation, and customer service.

As new principals accept the role of instructional leaders in schools, it is critical that they understand the roles and responsibilities of the LMS. A special training session, Georgia Media Specialist Evaluation Program, is conducted by the staff of the Department of Educational Media. The presentation covers the tenets addressed in *Information Power: Building Partnerships for Learning;* national, state, and local standards related to funding of library media programs; and computer and media technologies provided in library media centers.[16] We recommend that an LMS be appointed to the school's leadership team to provide support for these standards. At the end of the training, principals have expressed deep appreciation for the information presented and have often acknowledged their lack of knowledge about the components of effective library media programs and the criteria for evaluating an LMS.

Teachers benefit from professional learning activities planned and presented in schools by LMSs and at the school system level. School-based classes are offered on topics that are important to the school community and support the school improvement plan developed by the leadership team. A few topics are copyright compliance, effective strategies for Internet searching, information literacy standards and skills, and reading-related activities.

OBJECTIVES

The mission statement of our school system is "to guarantee that each learner develops individual potential and becomes a contributing citizen." The following objectives of the professional development program foster compliance with this mission:

> ➤ introduce or reinforce curricular-related information that supports the learning and teaching roles of the LMS
> ➤ introduce or reinforce media and computer technology skills that encourage authentic assessment of student learning
> ➤ provide opportunities for LMSs to demonstrate areas of expertise and successful program implementation by serving as instructors to LMS colleagues and teachers
> ➤ demonstrate collaboration between departments involved in professional learning activities

SCHOOL LIBRARY MEDIA SPECIALIST'S LEADERSHIP ROLE

LMSs and system-level library media coordinators are the primary instructors in professional learning classes. Topics range from Accelerated Reader to Zip Code searches on the Internet and are designed to meet the needs of the audience. Classes begin with basic foundational information and progress to advanced levels on a variety of topics. Instructors are expected to solicit evaluative comments from class members about content and instructional strategies employed during the sessions and identify needs and interests for future classes.

CONTRIBUTIONS TO STUDENT LEARNING

Peer-to-peer instruction is an effective model for professional learning in building a community of learners. Participants develop an appreciation of and support for fellow colleagues and receive new information and skills to assist students and teachers. This empowerment of LMSs is often the impetus for reevaluating the school library media program and its contributions to improving student achievement.

FUNDING

Funding for professional learning is provided by funds from the Georgia Department of Education through the Department of Professional Learning in the school system. Expenditures for supplies, stipends for instructors, and contracts for outside consultants for professional development classes are reported to and audited by the Department of Professional Learning.

EVALUATION

The formal evaluation of the professional learning classes is a five-point Likert scale that addresses content, presentation format, anticipated change of practice by the participant as a result of the class, and physical location of the class. Positive responses from participants generally hover between Strongly Agree and Agree.

Speak Softly and Carry a Big "Schtick"

SHARON BRUBAKER
H. M. BRADER ELEMENTARY SCHOOL, NEWARK, DELAWARE

In our media- and graphic-rich society, educators sometimes feel that we need to carry a big shtick when presenting information to students. A little drama hooks students into a unit of study, but our collaborative units at H. M. Brader Elementary are rooted firmly in the backward design concept of unit development.

We began this journey a little over seven years ago with the award of the Technology Literacy Challenge Fund Grant. This grant of $250,000 provided a staff writing specialist to take the library out of the unit count and transform our library to an open, flexibly scheduled library; an on-staff technology specialist; a paraprofessional for the library media center; and funds to help transform our school to a high-technology school. When this grant ended, we applied for the Enhancing Education Through Technology Grant to continue our program, as well as mentor two additional schools in Delaware with $150,000 used primarily to fund staffing. When grant funding ended, our administration, staff, and parent support assisted in the district to provide funds to continue our program.

When we began our flexible scheduled library program, staff trod lightly, entering into collaboration with slight trepidation. Within the year, over 90 percent of the staff looked enthusiastically forward to continuing collaborations the next year. We have not gone without growing pains, but the program has been overwhelmingly successful. Administration provided continued technology training and training in back-mapping as staff changed and grew with collaborative units.

Circulation statistics have skyrocketed since our program began (exhibit 2.8). Students from preschool to fifth grade, staff, and parents enjoy the ability to visit the library media center at any time for circulation and computing. Parents take advantage at drop-off and pickup times to drop by the library media center to

Year	Total Circulations	Total Holds Placed
2006	39,488	18
2005	64,606	84
2004	55,314	77
2003	51,623	116
2002	57,727	102
2001	47,068	260
2000	42,573	158
Total	358,399	815

EXHIBIT 2.8

LIBRARY CIRCULATION STATISTICS,
2000–2006

check out materials. Monthly family reading nights provide a cozy setting to listen to stories, read together, and check out materials to share with their children. Also, many parents volunteer their time to run Book Buddies or volunteer parent-led literature circle groups.

Working collaboratively is a process that takes time. Over the years, we continue to use the trash-n-treasure note-taking technique, described by Barbara Jensen as the ability to find the gems in the materials being reviewed, in unit development and redevelopment.[17]

A sense of humor and a little bit of chocolate don't hurt either! Our collaboration begins with the library media specialist and the classroom teacher. We seek collaboration with our district cadre, staff writing specialist, staff technology specialist, and others to brainstorm in the unit planning and teaching. With the backward design process, we whittle down to the essential big questions of what we would like students to learn and take away with them for lifelong learning. These questions and understandings are founded in our state standards. Brainstorming and discussion with the collaboration team result in strong essential questions. We refer to these constantly when planning activities for the unit and as a reminder to students and ourselves as we undertake the learning within each unit. With these essential questions in mind, we develop assessments.

With our active curriculum, we have turned from many pencil-and-paper assessments to observational assessments. In teaching information literacy, we use observational assessments of students using the electronic card catalog, electronic databases, and search engines effectively and trade and reference book resources as well. We have developed a rubric (exhibit 2.9) for use in assessment. The classroom teacher who is working collaboratively may use other assessments in the unit in the library media center or in the classroom setting. We also brainstorm as a group on additional rubrics to use for the unit and access rubrics from the Delaware Department of Education.

With these elements established, we begin to plan activities to reach the understanding and develop lessons where students can work fairly independently to reach their goals. We first try to hook students into the unit with a fun activity. In doing this, we also introduce the unit, the goals, and the big questions so that students understand what to expect within the unit. For example, some hooks have been for our writing specialist and library media specialist to use a fog machine and come back from the dead as they portrayed famous Americans for a biography unit. Our writing specialist dressed as Amelia Earhart and in a living history presentation presented information on her life and answered questions by students. The library media specialist became Georgia O'Keeffe for a day. In our Prodigious Polyhedra unit, students are wowed by looking at a presentation of polyhedral structures of the common cold; fifth disease, a viral illness that produces a distinctive red facial rash; and the ever-popular rotavirus (or throw-up virus). Looking at the platonic solid structures, we inform students that they are now the CEOs of the TIM5 Toy Company and need to design directions for staff to build polyhedral structures as blocks to sell. A treasure hunt kicks off an atlas and map unit. Our outdoor classroom provides a wonderful hook for units on organisms, plants, structure and function, Native American life, insects, and other topics. Nothing compares to the excitement of a frog hopping in front of a student, watching pond creatures swim in a small tank under the visual presenter and be displayed as "Tadpole TV," or watching the library media specialist get stuck in the mud or fall into the pond! Discovering

ISTE/Information Skills Rubric

LEVEL	Information Skills	ISTE Skills	Score
Information Skills "Proficient"	❏ I think about and extract details from several types of resources. ❏ I organize information in different ways. ❏ I usually remember to write a bibliography.	❏ I can use a variety of media and technology resources for independent learning. ❏ I can use technology tools. ❏ I can use input and output devices.	**3**
Information Skills "Essential"	❏ I can think about and write details from one type of information resource. ❏ I know some ways to organize information. ❏ I can use one or two organizers very well. ❏ Sometimes I write a bibliography.	❏ I know some ways to use media and technology resources. ❏ I need some assistance using technology tools. ❏ I can use input and output devices.	**2**
Information Skills "In Progress"	❏ I don't understand how to use information resources. ❏ I try to organize information, but I have trouble and I need to ask for help. ❏ I need to be reminded to write a bibliography.	❏ I have difficulty using a variety of media and technology resources. ❏ I cannot use technology tools without assistance. ❏ I have difficulty using input/output devices.	**1**

EXHIBIT 2.9 INFORMATION SKILLS RUBRIC

the elephant-like bark of a beech tree and watching a dragonfly emerge from its larval stage provide a rich base for learning.

Our community joined with us in our annual Frog Watch events where we gathered statistics for the National Wildlife Federation on frog populations. Listening to frogs, catching various amphibians, and touring the school woodlands and wetlands are a fun community weekly event from April until June.

When we have hooked the students into the unit, we begin to look at the best way to use the information resources. Building on the brainstorming from students, the library media specialist teaches information skills through a variety of minilessons using the Big6 information-solving process developed by Mike Eisenberg and Bob Berkowitz, using the electronic catalog, search engines and databases, and print resources.[18] The lessons are complemented with songs, kinesthetic activities, and hands-on practice. Students are reminded of the big question and premises for the unit.

With this established, students begin their research, and the teachers and library media specialist become the facilitators. Excitement buzzes throughout the library media center as students find cool facts and interesting information. Students peer-teach and share website information and recommendations for good print resources. Depending on the unit, students begin their final project in the library, the classroom, or at home. Many times we hold celebrations in the library media center, the classroom, or with grade levels when projects are completed. Student work is displayed throughout the school and posted on our website.

With the strong vision of collaboration from our school administration and the collegial environment of the staff, the process of best practices and high standards for student achievement becomes less a chore and more of a challenge that can be met more easily than being a sage on the stage in the solo classroom environment.

Collaborating with Advanced Placement U.S. Government Teachers

ANNA MARIA MENZA
CHERRY CREEK HIGH SCHOOL, GREENWOOD VILLAGE, COLORADO

SUMMARY

Breakthroughs in collaboration can occur when teacher-librarians strategically place themselves in unlikely circles. Two teacher-librarians began a yearlong collaboration with the Advanced Placement (AP) U.S. Government teachers at their school as a result of attending an AP Institute.

Two of the most recent additions to the Cherry Creek High School (CCHS) teacher-librarian team were equally intrigued by the prospect of attending the AP Institute, held annually on their home site, in August 2005. They quickly decided on AP U.S. Government when they learned that their own social studies coordinator, one of the four AP U.S. Government teachers, was the instructor for the four-day session. Neither this highly regarded teacher nor her team had found much time in the past for scheduled library research due to the time constraints of teaching the curriculum in one semester.

SCHOOL LIBRARY MEDIA SPECIALIST'S LEADERSHIP ROLE

The teacher-librarians set out to prove that teacher-librarian involvement in AP U.S. Government was essential, but they kept their expectations realistic. They quickly learned that teaching AP U.S. Government in one semester is a monumental task. The workshop proved rich in content and best practices for teaching it and was unlike anything else that either of the librarians had ever attended.

The other participants, all AP U.S. Government teachers, seemed impressed that two teacher-librarians would sit through four days of subject-specific instruction. Both teacher-librarians did their best to impart to the AP teachers that they could also work with their teacher-librarians to identify and analyze sources for students to use in preparing debates and term papers. When everyone parted, the teacher-librarians did not know if they had accomplished their goal, but they definitely had new insight into the AP U.S. Government curriculum.

Imagine the surprise and delight of the teacher-librarians when they received a call in early September from one of the AP U.S. Government teachers. He said, "I know that you went to the AP Institute and know what we do and we wondered if you could help us gather some sources for the major term paper." He added that he had the prompt in hand and hoped to get started right away. Fortunately, the timing worked for one of the teacher-librarians who had attended the institute to meet with him. She was already starting to sense victory.

A successful collaboration began that established the teacher-librarians as the research experts who could support the AP teachers as content experts. This entailed the librarian's ability to listen to the teachers' needs and expectations and then identify resource materials that would support the assignment given to the students. This partnership of the AP teachers as content experts and the teacher-librarians as resource experts helped the AP teachers focus on the high volume of lesson planning and grading that the AP team faced. The end result, an instructional site that aggregated the assignment and resources in one place, exceeded the expectations of the AP teachers so much that they set aside a period for the librarian to present it to the students. (Interested teachers and librarians can view the site at http://www.cchs.ccsd.k12.co.us/academics/class_projects/APUSGov/ ap_us_gov_index.html.)

School libraries should strive to serve all students. AP classes provide one vehicle for reaching many hardworking, high-achieving students. Cherry Creek High School's philosophy of offering AP courses to as many students willing to take them is aligned with the College Board's commitment "to the principle that all students deserve an opportunity to participate in rigorous and academically challenging courses and programs." School administration, faculty, and staff believe that this philosophy sets a standard of excellence for the entire school. Providing research support to AP classes gives the library a chance to contribute to the climate of high expectations for all at CCHS.

It was clear that the AP teachers had little time to participate other than attending the first meeting and signing off on the sources. A librarian who attended the institute took the lead on gathering electronic sources from the databases due to the currency of the topic and started to aggregate them. The teacher-librarian understood that she might not even have the opportunity to give the students a presentation on the databases, so she set out to make an instructional site that was self-explanatory. Also, she realized that it would serve ten sections of students, so it had to be clear and concise. Keeping in mind that the teachers had merely handed out hard copies of articles in the past, the librarian knew that content prevailed over the research process in this case. However, she knew that with her guidance and explicit directions the students would be navigating through several databases. She showed a draft of the site to the teachers and explained that they could introduce it to the students themselves during class with very little time lost. She also said that she was willing to visit each classroom after the paper was assigned for a brief follow-up to get student feedback on any confusion or glitches they encountered. The AP teachers surprised the teacher-librarians when they came back with the suggestion that the teacher-librarian present the site to their classes in the library. The library team was able to accommodate every section in one day by doubling them up some periods in the large community rooms adjoining the library. Everyone on the library staff played a part, from the technology specialist who helped post the website to the clerks who set up the chairs for the large classes.

CONTRIBUTIONS TO STUDENT ACHIEVEMENT

The experience led to collaboration with some of the school's hardest-working students because they learned that they could rely on the teacher-librarians to help them navigate the databases, cite sources, and get a little moral support when they felt overwhelmed. CCHS library will continue to strengthen its support of AP classes because both teacher-librarians enrolled in the AP Institute for English Language for summer 2006, fully encouraged by the rest of the library team.

FUNDING

CCHS paid the AP Institute Early Bird Registration fee of $525 for each teacher-librarian with staff development funds. The collaboration between teachers and librarians, site creation, and its implementation took place during regular school hours and did not require additional funding.

EVALUATION

The teacher-librarians knew they were successful when the AP teachers reported that this was one of the best term papers ever assigned based on the support given to the students with all of the sources aggregated in one place and on the quality of the papers. The social studies coordinator even scored one paper with a rare 100 percent. Further evidence of success came when the AP teachers asked the teacher-librarians to develop another site for the second term paper. (For the second site, go to http://www.cchs.ccsd.k12.co.us/academics/class_projects/APUSGov2/2ndpaper.htm.)

AP U.S. Government was offered again for the second semester, and the teacher already informed the library that he plans to use the instructional sites for term papers. Evidence that the social studies coordinator now regards the teacher-librarians as research experts to the AP program came with her most recent request for help locating articles to support the major term paper for AP Comparative Government that she teaches second semester.

NOTES

1. "ALA/AASL Standards for School Library Media Specialists," in *The Whole School Library Handbook,* edited by Blanche Woolls and David V. Loertscher (Chicago: American Library Association, 2005), 168.
2. Patricia O'Brien Libutti, "Model Organizational Structure and Best Practices for Successful National Collaborative Information Partnerships" (paper presented at the U.S. Education Information Network Kick-off Conference, Washington, DC, November 13–14, 1997), ERIC Document Reproduction Service ED414905.
3. "Mind Styles: Anthony Gregorc," n.d., retrieved August 3, 2007, from http://web.cortland.edu/andersmd/learning/Gregorc.htm.
4. Melody Thomas, "What Is Collaboration to You?" in *School Library Management,* 5th ed., edited by Catherine Andronik (Worthington, OH: Linworth Publishing, 2003), 47–48.

5. Patricia Potter Wilson and Josette Anne Lyders, *Leadership for Today's School Library: A Handbook for the School Library Media Specialist and the School Principal* (Westport, CT: Greenwood Press, 2001), 35–44.

6. Norman Webb and Carol Doll, "Contributions of Library Power to Collaborations between Teachers and Librarians." *School Libraries Worldwide* 5, no. 2 (1999): 29.

7. Wilson and Lyders, *Leadership for Today's School Library*, 53–57.

8. Grant P. Wiggins and Jay McTighe, *Understanding by Design*, 2nd ed. (Alexandria, VA: Association for Supervision and Curriculum Development, 2005).

9. Michael Eisenberg and Robert Berkowitz, *The Big6* (1987). Retrieved August 3, 2007, from http://www.big6.com.

10. Wiggins and McTighe, *Understanding by Design*.

11. "Powerful Partnerships: Partnerships for Powerful Learning," rev. ed. (Hilliard, OH: Hilliard City School District, K–12 Media Program Course of Study, 2006), p. x.

12. Ibid.

13. Joyce Kasman Valenza, *Power Tools: 100+ Essential Forms and Presentations for Your School Library Information Program* (Chicago: American Library Association, 1998), form 3.10.

14. Ibid., form 2.1. Sandra Hughes-Hasslee and Anne Wheelock (eds.), *The Information-Powered School* (Chicago: American Library Association, 2001), 51.

15. Donald C. Adcock (ed.), *A Planning Guide for Information Power Building Partnerships for Learning: Building Partners for Learning with School Library Media Program Assessment Rubric for the 21st Century* (Chicago: American Association of School Librarians, 1999).

16. American Association of School Librarians, Association for Educational Communications and Technology, *Information Power: Building Partnerships for Learning* (Chicago: American Library Association, 1998).

17. Barbara Jensen, "Reading for Information: The Trash-N-Treasure Method of Teaching Note-Taking," retrieved January 30, 2008, from http://lsit.coe.ecu.edu/project/treasure.htm.

18. Eisenberg and Berkowitz, *The Big6*.

CHAPTER 3

Leadership in Information Access and Delivery

*I*nformation access begins with the collection. The school library media center collection, whether physical or virtual, needs to support the curriculum and expand learning opportunities for students. The collaboration that underlies teaching and learning can be enhanced by the involvement of classroom teachers in collection development. This involvement increases the use of library resources for instruction, promotes flexible access to the library, and contributes to curriculum development throughout the school year.[1]

The involvement of classroom teachers in collection development can foster a collection development policy that serves as the curriculum guide for the library as well as the guide to the curriculum of the school. As discussed in chapter 2, leadership in teaching and learning requires knowledge of the goals and curriculum of the school and district. This collaboration with teachers will extend the knowledge of these goals and curriculum and support an analysis of the collection to meet curriculum needs.

David V. Loertscher provides a curriculum mapping model to guide school library media specialists in analyzing the needs of the school and evaluating the strengths and gaps of the collection in meeting those needs.[2] This taxonomy of the school library media program supports resource-based teaching as well as the taxonomies for learning detailed by Lorin Anderson and David Krathwohl.[3]

In 1956, Benjamin S. Bloom developed and published a classification scheme of student learning in six major categories: knowledge, comprehension, application, analysis, synthesis, and evaluation. Anderson and Krathwohl's taxonomy builds on Bloom's work but also includes a focus on the emerging role of the learner as a content creator as well as a content consumer. This new taxonomy contains four knowledge dimensions (factual knowledge, conceptual knowledge, procedural knowledge, and metacognitive knowledge), as well as six cognitive process dimensions (remember, understand, apply, analyze, evaluate, and create).[4] These new knowledge dimensions are critical to learning today, with its emphasis on the full integration of information literacy and resource-based learning.

The availability of shared electronic collections such as those provided by state departments of education should be included in any analysis of the library's collection. The applicability of quality Internet resources appropriate to specific age groups that have been collected through WebQuests (http://webquest.org/index.php) and the Librarians' Internet Index (http://lii.org) may also be appropriate to include in any collection analysis. Online collections of children's literature such as the International Children's Digital Library (http://www.icdlbooks.org) may also meet the teaching and learning goals of the school or district. When these online resources are appropriate to the needs of the school or district, easy access should be provided for them, and these resources should be considered part of the school library media center collection.

The ever-expanding nature of shared collections and the availability of quality Internet resources have changed the definition of library collections. Knowing the local collection remains important, but knowing the needs of users in order to match those needs to local and electronic resources is critical, as illustrated by Katherine Lowe of Boston Arts Academy/Fenway High School.

The impact of remote access in meeting the information access needs of teachers is met through the professional library of the DeKalb County (Georgia) School System.

Access to local and electronic collections has traditionally been provided through card and electronic catalogs and indexes and databases. However, these tools are not structured to parallel the curriculum. The school library media specialist focus on the curriculum may require moving beyond traditional methods of organization and access. In one school library media center that I visited, a schoolwide emphasis on the use of the Accelerated Reader program was reflected by the arrangement of Accelerated Reader titles by reading level rather than by Dewey Decimal classification. The emphasis on resource lists on specific topics that are a feature of many websites established by school and school district libraries that have received the NSLMPY Award is another way to provide access beyond the online catalog.

Another consideration in providing collection access is serving the needs of all students. Although the traditional ways of access may meet the needs of logical and sequential thinkers, school library media programs also need to appeal to those whose learning style is intuitive and tactile. Donna W. Brown has described the steps needed to appeal to all types of learners in her article, "Libraries Can Be Right Brained."[5] Her recommendations to appeal to the holistic, random, nonverbal, and intuitive styles of the right-brained learner may be met through the development of displays. Another approach to meeting the needs of the right-brained student is through the development of websites, an approach described by Pam Strom of New Trier High School as well as the DeKalb County project outlined by Patricia Pickard.

Library Research Tutorial

KATHERINE LOWE
BOSTON ARTS ACADEMY/FENWAY HIGH SCHOOL LIBRARY AND BOSTON SYMPHONY
ORCHESTRA EDUCATION RESOURCE CENTER, BOSTON, MASSACHUSETTS

Students are required to access information from a variety of sources for major research projects to ensure that they are using quality print and online subscription resources along with information they find on the Internet. For a tenth-grade humanities project comparing Boston's immigrant groups, students must locate a minimum of eleven sources: a primary source of any type, seven

---

As you complete this tutorial, you will find:

1 *article* from a reference book about your immigrant group
1 *nonfiction book* about your immigrant group
1 *primary source* by a person from your immigrant group

You will write down the sources you find in your Source Log. Write the name of your immigrant group below, along with as many terms as you can think of to describe that group. (For example: Puerto Ricans, Puerto Rican Americans, Hispanic Americans, Latinos)

_____ _____ _____ _____

_____ _____ _____ _____

_____ _____ _____ _____

To find an article from a reference book using web catalog

1. Start at the *Library web page*.

2. Click on *Web Catalog*.

3. Click on *School Access*. (If you are not at school, you must use the *Home Access* link.)

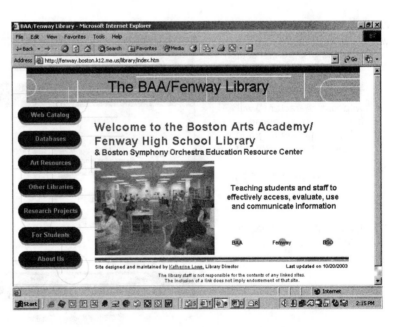

EXHIBIT 3.1

LIBRARY RESEARCH TUTORIAL FOR THE IMMIGRATION PROJECT

nonfiction or reference books, one article from a subscription database, one newspaper or magazine article, and a website or one other source chosen by the student.

We developed a tutorial to teach students some advanced methods of searching the library's online catalog, how to combine keywords and phrases to narrow a search, and how to use truncation (exhibit 3.1). Students document citation information on a source list and use information they have gathered to present an exhibition using visual displays, performance, and text to show how their own ancestors' immigrant group compares to another group that settled in the Boston area.

4. Next, click on *Search Catalog*.

5. Change the drop-down menu at the left of the first search box to *Subject*.

6. Type *immigra**. (Using the wildcard character (*) will find more items because it will search for *immigration*, *immigrant*, or *immigrants*.)

7. In the second search box, change the drop-down menu to *Call Number*.

8. Type *ref* (for reference) in the search box.

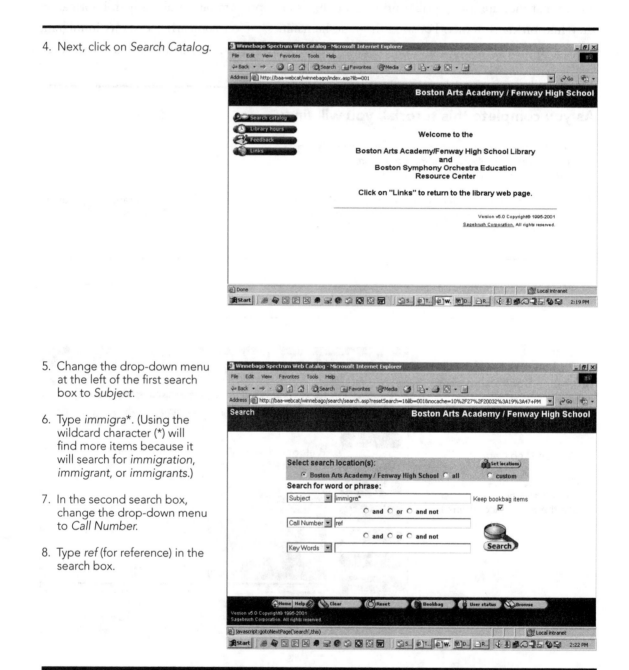

EXHIBIT 3.1 - CONTINUED

LIBRARY RESEARCH TUTORIAL FOR THE IMMIGRATION PROJECT

Your search will locate many reference books that have information about immigrants and immigration. Some will have more information about your immigrant group than others. Take some time to select the best ones by clicking on the titles and reading the summaries of each book.

9. Write the call numbers for the books that look the most useful below.

_____   _____   _____   _____

_____   _____   _____   _____

_____   _____   _____   _____

10. Find these books in the reference section of the library.

11. Look up the different names you listed for your immigrant group in the index of each reference book or reference set.

12. Find one good article about your immigrant group and make a copy of it on the library's copier (10 cents/page).

13. Write down the citation information for the book your article came from on your Source Log.

To find a nonfiction book using web catalog

1. Leaving the drop-down menus on *Key Words*, type three different names for your immigrant group into the search boxes.
2. Use the wildcard character (*) to increase the number of items you will find.
3. Click "*or*" between the search boxes to search for all three different immigrant group names at once.

This search will yield several sources.

4. Write down the call numbers for the books that look the most useful to you, and then choose one book to use for this assignment.

_____   _____   _____   _____

_____   _____   _____   _____

_____   _____   _____   _____

5. On your Source Log, write the citation information for the book you chose.

To find a primary source using web catalog

What kind of primary source would you like to find? A letter? A memoir? An autobiography? A song? A diary? A journal? A photograph? A poem?

1. Make a list of the types of primary sources you want to find. List several so if you don't find one, you will have other options.

_____   _____   _____   _____

_____   _____   _____   _____

_____   _____   _____   _____

2. In the first two search boxes, write two of the terms above.

3. Click "or" in between the two search boxes.

4. In the third search box, type the name of your immigrant group.

5. Click "and" between the second and third search boxes.

6. Remember to use the wildcard character (*) to increase your results.

7. Repeat your search as many times as necessary, using different combinations of primary sources and immigrant group names in the search boxes.

8. After performing several searches, you will have found quite a few primary sources in both circulating books and reference books.

9. Write the call numbers below for the sources you want to look at.

_____   _____   _____   _____

_____   _____   _____   _____

_____   _____   _____   _____

10. Choose a primary document from one of the sources you found and make a copy of the document.

11. On your Source Log, write the citation information for the book containing the primary source document you chose.

EXHIBIT 3.1 - CONTINUED

LIBRARY RESEARCH TUTORIAL FOR THE IMMIGRATION PROJECT

Library Website Creation

PAM STROM
NEW TRIER HIGH SCHOOL—WINNETKA CAMPUS, WINNETKA, ILLINOIS

SUMMARY

New Trier librarians recognized that students who were drawn to more graphically appealing websites were routinely overlooking the high-quality resources on the text-intensive school library media center's website. As a result of collaboration between the librarians and the technology staff, a more readily accessible website was created. This project was the result of student and teacher input regarding how best to promote the use of the library website, which contains multiple subscription databases, websites evaluated and selected by the school library media specialists, and the online catalog. Once the need was assessed, the technology staff worked with librarians to create a user-friendly interface that was far more visual than the previous text-intensive site. This work between librarians and the technology staff took place in coordination with an ongoing discussion regarding the library's needs, how best to encourage student and teacher use of library resources, and how the newly designed website could be better used during library instruction to engage students and develop information literacy skills (see http://www.newtrier.k12.il.us/library/default.htm).

OBJECTIVE

The major objective of this project was to make the website more user friendly, recognizing the needs of students interested more in the visual world and connecting them with high-quality resources the library offers. New Trier's motto is, "Minds to inquiry, hearts to compassion, and lives to the service of humanity." This project better enables students to access "minds to inquiry."

SCHOOL LIBRARY MEDIA SPECIALIST'S LEADERSHIP ROLE

The librarians researched numerous websites for design and user-friendly potential before creating their own website. The librarians in this project were indispensable to the overall creation of the website, working with the technology staff while effectively using both Dreamweaver and Fireworks software in the process.

CONTRIBUTIONS TO STUDENT ACHIEVEMENT

This project helps students and teachers gain better access to the library's resources. Putting a fresh face on the library's website has increased awareness and knowledge of databases, credibility of sources, and more. In turn, students produce higher-quality products and build on their ability to evaluate information.

FUNDING

This was a yearlong project funded through an individual technology learning plan grant that the school sponsors. Total hours spent on the project cannot be calculated exactly, but an individual

$500 stipend was given to two library media specialists with three school days allotted per librarian for release time. It was an intense endeavor that superseded the structured release time allotted.

EVALUATION

The project was initially evaluated by students in focus groups, who approved overwhelmingly of the design and the user-friendly approach to the library's resources. Daily, the project is used by classroom teachers, individual students, administrators, and the community. Teachers also continually ask librarians to update important links to individual teacher assignment websites that the library is responsible for maintaining.

Remote Access @ your library

PATRICIA PICKARD
DEKALB COUNTY SCHOOL SYSTEM, DECATUR, GEORGIA

PROFESSIONAL LIBRARY

Under the direction of the state Department of Educational Media, the Professional Library has a theme of information and access that supports teachers and administrators of the DeKalb County System School in their educational pursuits. The Professional Library is classified as a special library with a large metropolitan school system. It consists of approximately fourteen thousand book holdings, an extensive ERIC document collection, grant-writing resources, periodicals, and electronic databases. The library is a governing member of the Southeastern Library Network, Inc. (SOLINET), a nonprofit library consortium serving the southeastern United States, working in partnership with libraries to improve access to information, and Georgia OnLine Database (GOLD). GOLD serves as the interlibrary lending and union listing system used throughout the state. Its consortium comprises approximately two hundred academic, public, private, school, special, and technical college libraries. GOLD has group accessibility, which operates through the Online Computer Library Center (OCLC) and OCLC WorldCat database. Through the SOLINET and GOLD consortia, the Professional Library has information access to search worldwide for educational resources using the WorldCat database. Resources are obtained through interlibrary loan from within the state of Georgia, the Southeast, as well as nationally and internationally.

Educators of the DeKalb County School System also have access to the teacher certification preparation study guides and microfiche. Teachers and administrators can access the Professional Library remotely at http://plibrary.dekalb.k12.ga.us at all times. The Professional Library website allows accessibility to the online catalog, professional journal finder database, research database, and links to professional organizations. Three databases (Access World News, Foundations Grant Directory, and ProQuest) require a password for remote access. The librarian has integrated these password-protected databases and password-free electronic resources into GALILEO, Georgia's virtual library, for efficient information access. Teachers and administrators e-mail or phone in their requests to the Professional Library staff.

LEARNING RESOURCES CENTER

The learning resources center (LRC), under the direction of the Department of Educational Media, provides access to its collection of approximately thirteen thousand items in VHS, DVD, CD, and sheet music formats. It supports pre-K–12 instruction. Teachers and administrators may search the MediaNet catalog to locate and reserve an audiovisual title using software designed by Dymaxion Research, Nova Scotia, Canada. Once the item is reserved using the educator's special client code number and password, the LRC staff verify the availability of the item. The item is sent and returned by intersystem courier. MediaNet is available at all times.

OBJECTIVES

The objective of information access and delivery is in compliance with strategy 2 of the systemwide strategic plan: "We will guarantee the effectiveness of administrative and instructional staff." Reference and staff development services on Internet training and information access delivery systems are a large part of our mission to supply the professional educational needs of school system teachers, administrators, and staff.

The district professional librarian provides professional learning activities in electronic database search and Professional Library services. Ongoing training is offered to instructional staff on GALILEO, which constantly evolves to meet the information needs of Georgia's students.

SCHOOL LIBRARY MEDIA SPECIALIST'S LEADERSHIP ROLE

The district professional librarian's role is to assess the needs of teachers and administrators and develop and manage the collection to address educators' needs. Evaluation of the services and resources provided by the Professional Library is provided through the analysis of statistics, as well as through qualitative comments provided by teachers and administrators about the quality of services received from the Professional Library.

CONTRIBUTIONS TO STUDENT ACHIEVEMENT

The staff of the Department of Educational Media empower teachers and administrators with access and delivery to cultivate their knowledge in contributing to student achievement. The access to electronic resources at the Professional Library website puts current information and research results at the fingertips of educators. This delivery of information allows classroom teachers to research instructional strategies that address the immediate needs of students and maximize the teachable moment.

EVALUATION

Evaluation of the services and resources provided by the Professional Library is qualitative through comments and notes shared by teachers and administrators about the services received from the library. Quantitative evaluation, including quarterly statistics, is furnished through the following areas:

Professional Library

➤ Periodicals and books circulated

➤ Interlibrary loan requests for school library media specialists

➤ Electronic database use

➤ Reference assistance, including phone calls, walk-ins, and e-mails

➤ Hours of professional learning activities provided by the district Professional Library

Learning Resources Center

➤ Bookings shipped

➤ Remote bookings

➤ Mediagraphy search hits

➤ Catalog search hits

NOTES

1. Diane McAfee Hopkins, "School Library Collection: An Essential Building Block," *School Libraries Worldwide* 5, no. 2 (1999): 1–15.

2. David V. Loertscher, *Taxonomies of the School Library Media Program,* 2nd ed. (San Jose, CA: Hi Willow Press, 2000).

3. Lorin Anderson and David R. Krathwohl, *A Taxonomy for Learning, Teaching, and Assessing: A Revision of Bloom's Taxonomy of Educational Objectives* (New York: Longman, 2001).

4. Benjamin S. Bloom (ed.), *Taxonomy of Educational Objectives: The Classification of Educational Goals by a Committee of College and University Examiners* (New York: Longman, Green, 1956); Anderson and Krathwohl, *A Taxonomy for Learning, Teaching, and Assessing.*

5. Donna W. Brown, "Libraries Can Be Right-Brained," in *School Library Management,* 5th ed., edited by Catherine Andronik (Worthington, OH: Linworth Publishing, 2003), 133–134.

CHAPTER 4

Leadership in Program Administration

The school library media specialist's role as a program administrator requires the application of multifaceted skills in support of finance and budgeting activities, facilities management, program organization, staffing leadership and management, and public relations. Success as a program administrator is essential to successful delivery of the school library media center services that support the school library media specialists' roles in teaching and learning and information access and delivery.

Finance and Budgeting

"Show me the money" was the catchphrase of the 1996 motion picture *Jerry McGuire*. Principals, superintendents, school boards, and others who determine funds for school library media centers might adapt this phrase to, "Show me *the reasons for* the money." "The key to budgeting is that the budget process is a setting of priorities and that every school has some discretionary funds. So to obtain the funds you need, first you must ask, and then you must focus your requests on the budget holder's priorities."[1]

The complex nature of school library media centers is reflected in the multiple categories that should be reflected in developing a budget for it:

➤ supplies for materials processing, communication, and audiovisual equipment support

➤ books, periodicals, and multimedia materials to support the curriculum

➤ books, periodicals, and multimedia materials that are part of the on-site professional collection

➤ online databases

➤ binding and repair of materials

➤ audiovisual and computer equipment to provide access to the collection and support library functions

➤ equipment repairs and cleaning

➤ support costs and maintenance agreements for library systems software for circulation and cataloging

➤ supplies, honoraria, and other funding for promotional materials and events

➤ professional development funds, including conference registrations and travel

➤ professional organization membership fees

Requests in each of these budget categories need to conform to the model used by the district and should be based on needs assessment and relevant data. These data may include comparison of the school's budget to local, state, and national standards, as well as data on the impact of the school library media center on student achievement. Information on national trends in funding for school library media centers is provided each January by *School Library Journal*. In addition, studies on the impact of quality school library media centers are available at the Library Research Service website (http://www.lrs.org).

Although national trends in funding and national studies on the impact of school library media centers may serve as excellent background information for school library media specialists, they should also remember the words of former Speaker of the House Tip O'Neill: "All politics is local." Principals, superintendents, and school boards want to know the impact of the school library media center on *their* students. The Wisconsin Educational Media and Technology Associations, WEMAtter Toolkit (http://www.wemaonline.org/ab.wematter.datacollection.cfm) provides access to many resources to guide in data collection on the impact of individual school library media programs. Because the school library media center's budget is often considered part of the overall school or district budget, information on how its request will support or align with the needs of other programs will demonstrate a commitment to collaboration rather than foster internal competition.

Principals, superintendents, and other decision makers also want to be confident of the accuracy of the budget request. Many of the factors for successful collaboration outlined in chapter 2 also apply to the budget development process. Accuracy in budget requests will establish trust and engender respect. The development of a multiyear spending plan to account for the costs of major recurring purchases such as computers, databases, and equipment will assist decision makers in their budget planning and help the school library media specialist establish credibility.

In recent years, the twin factors of accountability and concerns about high taxes have led to an increase in state control of budgets in many states. The school library media specialist needs to know which allocation and budget decisions are made at the state, district, and school levels. The governmental level at which budget decisions are made may well affect the level of influence of the individual school library media specialist. As allocation and budget decisions are made at the district, regional, or state level, collaboration with other school library media specialists may become an increasingly effective strategy.

In presenting the budget request to any governmental level, clear communication is essential. All requests should be succinct, contain little jargon, and delineate the impact of the request on the goals and priorities of the school, district, or state. Asking for a specific amount per student instead of a lump sum focuses the request on student learning rather than on the overall cost of the request.

Facilities

The management of facilities and equipment is another aspect of the program administration responsibilities of the school library media specialist. Facilities management requires constant monitoring of the space to make certain that the arrangement, decor, and organization of the space support the school's instructional goals and create a welcoming space for students and others. Libraries need to be "inviting to the mind, body and soul" in order to support a holistic view of student learning.[2]

One way in which to make certain that the library media center meets the needs of students is to ensure that the space and its furnishings support flexible use. At the 2006 *School Library Journal* Summit, Joan Frye Williams discussed the value of leaving library furnishings in the locations where they are moved by students as a way to demonstrate a commitment to student-centered design.[3] Student-centered design must also consider the diversity of needs that results from differences in the age range, physical abilities, and attributes of the intended users.

School library media specialists need to be cautious in using or responding to plans that rely exclusively on State Department of Education guidelines for space allocations for school library media centers. These may not reflect the realities of new technologies and the instructional role of the school library media center.[4] Evaluation of these guidelines should be made with an understanding that there is a "clear interaction between space and the degree to which they [school library media centers] implemented flexible scheduling."[5]

Elements to be included in a design plan for school library media centers may include multimedia production space, informal teaching and learning spaces, spaces for collections and equipment, service desks, teaching spaces, consulting space, group and individual study spaces, storytelling space, presentation spaces for students, office space for school library media staff, and work space for school library media center program administration activities. The appropriateness of these spaces to the needs of the school library media center should be evaluated as a regular part of the administration of the school library media program, not just in preparation for facilities development or remodeling. A "library walk-about checklist" developed by McGhee and Jansen can serve as a guide to this evaluation.[6] One example of evaluating a library media center to meet new and emerging needs is outlined by Maggie Schmude of New Trier High School.

The increasing emphasis on students as content creators, the availability of electronic catalogs and databases, and the appeal of multimedia resources to a variety of learning styles speaks to the importance of planning for technology in school library media center facilities. Donna Helvering, director of library services for the Millard, Nebraska, Public Schools (the 2003 NSLMPY Award winner), describes the impact of increased technology access on this district:

> Wireless access within buildings and fiber connectivity have enabled students to take advantage of video streaming technologies and increased network speed. Every teacher now has a new laptop computer to use for presentations, administrative tasks, communication and research. The staff is empowered to be more efficient teachers and model good information and technology skills for students. The Library Media Department plays a large role in this

technology infusion as staff developers, as coaches, as role models, and problem solvers. The media specialists are . . . the teachers who integrate technology in the content areas.[7]

The importance of collaboration with technology staff is described by Patricia Pickard of the DeKalb County System schools.

Organization

Flexible scheduling affects the facility needs of the school library media center. More important, "one of the hallmarks of a fully realized school library program is flexible scheduling," which contributes to higher student achievement.[8] This concept is eloquently stated by Douglas L. Zweizig: "A key premise of Library Power is that library facilities and resources can support instruction best if they are available at a time when they are most suited to a lesson or when spontaneous interests arise."[9]

Despite research on the value of flexible scheduling, teachers may view moving from fixed scheduling as loss of a planning period, so change may need to be gradual as teachers become familiar with flexible scheduling: "In one school, for example, half-classes visit the library for half a period, allowing for better attention for students in the library and giving the teacher a smaller group to work with in the classroom" (p. 19).[10]

Flexible scheduling will have an impact not only on student achievement but also on the staffing required for the school library media center. "The presence of support staff has been noted as necessary for a library to be responsive to multiple and spontaneous demands for service."[11]

Working with Staff and Volunteers

Responding to multiple and spontaneous demands for service will require school library media specialists to develop skills in working with other staff and with volunteers. These skills require an understanding of the difference between management and leadership. Program administration is concerned with managing the program, but school library media specialists who work with other staff and with volunteers must be focused on leading people. Leading people to reach the common goal of the school library media center can be aided by recognizing and following the principles of engagement:

1. Let go of negative opinions.
2. Make sure employees have the tools to do their jobs.
3. Provide clear expectations of values and vision.
4. Know employee goals and stressors and how employees define success.
5. Train and retrain in problem solving.
6. Ask how "you" are doing.
7. Pay attention to stories and rituals.
8. Reward and recognize in meaningful ways.
9. Be consistent.[12]

Leading staff and volunteers begins with following these principles. However, school library media specialists also need to manage the tasks of the school library media center and match them with available staff and volunteers.

Advocacy and Public Relations

Internal public relations activities are described in chapter 2 as part of the process of building collaborative relationships. The development of public relations activities targeted to audiences outside the school can serve to strengthen the program of the school library media center and boost the reputation of the school in the community. Collaboration with public libraries can extend the reach of both organizations, as well as provide a lesson to students on the value of lifelong learning. Working with the parent-teacher organization can demonstrate the value of the school library media center to parents and demonstrate a partnership between the school and the home.

This commitment to leadership requires a commitment to promoting the reputation of the school and the school library media program. The American Library Association's @ your library campaign provides a ready-made, widely recognized structure for these public relations activities. This added prominence for a school library media center may also aid in providing the school board, parents, and community with a deeper understanding of the changed role of the school library media specialist. Presenting this image includes the importance of demonstrating the school library media specialist's role as the place where the disparate subject and grade levels of the school are connected.[13] This connection promotes not the school library media center but the importance of this connection to student achievement.

Once the school library media center's message is connected to student achievement, the common value shared by school boards, businesses, parents, and the community, there are many ways in which the center can publicize its contributions. These include face-to-face opportunities such as hosting the district's board meeting; making presentations to the board, businesses, and the parent-teacher organization; and taking advantage of formal and informal networking opportunities. The face of the school library media center can also be presented through a "fast facts" flier; welcome packets to new teachers, students, and their parents; brochures; library newsletters; annual reports; and a robust website. Special events are an opportunity to highlight the role of the school library media center. These may include national events such as School Library Media Month or local events such as back-to-school night.[14]

These public relations activities are one part of developing a full advocacy plan. Public relations activities are a way of telling the community about the contributions of the school library media center. Marketing requires a focus on the needs of the audience and helps determine communication strategies.[15] Additional guidance in developing a public relations plan for school library media centers is provided by the AASL Advocacy Toolkit (available at http://www.ala.org/ala/aasl/aaslproftools/toolkits/aasladvocacy.cfm).

In "Advocacy and Public Relations Matters," Patricia Pickard delivers an overview of print and online resources that gives the public ownership in their programs.

Strategies for recruiting and working with volunteers as integral members of the school library media center staff are presented by Diane H. Thompson, while Patricia Pickard reviews her district's successful orientation and mentoring program for new school library media specialists.

Involvement of the community in the redesign of the school library media center is detailed by Maggie Schmude. Other ways of involving the community are provided in a description of programming for parents written by Kristin McKeown and in scenarios outlining the development of strong collaborative relationships with the public library by Patricia Pickard and Mary Trenerry and Stephanie Beisch.

The role of the school library media center in assisting individual schools in implementing the technology that is best for their students is the focus of Patricia Pickard's "Doing the Best We Can with the Technology We Have."

Flexible scheduling can be a key element of successful library programs; Janie Kossak discusses the advocacy process for making it part of the organization of the school, and Patricia Pickard reviews how the use of online communication tools can foster its implementation.

Donna Helvering provides an illustration of the use of good financing, budget, and advocacy practices that resulted in a doubling of her school library media center's budget, and Anne O'Malley discusses the importance of year-round integrated programming to the success of the New Trier High School library media center.

Advocacy and Public Relations Matters

PATRICIA PICKARD
DEKALB COUNTY SCHOOL SYSTEM, DECATUR, GEORGIA

SUMMARY

In the DeKalb County School System, "student achievement is the bottom line."[16] The Department of Educational Media is acutely aware of the need for advocacy and public relations to our success. A number of advocacy and public relations strategies boost the awareness of the essential contributions libraries make to student achievement within the system and into the school communities.

PUBLICATIONS FOR MANY AUDIENCES

A color brochure was designed and distributed to each school for use in promoting library media center (LMC) programs among parents. This brochure highlights significant Colorado, Texas, and Pennsylvania studies supporting increased student achievement with high-quality LMC programs. Services offered to local LMCs by the system-level Department of Educational Media are also outlined. Parents are referred to the American Library Association website so they will be prepared with the right questions to ask about the LMC on a visit to their child's school.

The Professional Library staff produces a new color brochure each year for DeKalb teachers and staff members. The library supports educational inquiry with fourteen thousand books, ERIC documents, interlibrary loan, and access to journals in print, on microfiche, and in online databases. The Professional Library's on-site remote access services, available all of the time, are listed along with specific URLs, hours, and a directional map.

A Learning Resources Center (LRC) brochure explains procedures for use of its collection of thirteen thousand items in CD, DVD, VHS, and sheet music formats and is available to all DeKalb teachers and staff.

The Link for Library Literacy is a new newsletter targeted to DeKalb administrators promoting LMC activities and services. LMC activities and services and library media specialist (LMS) honors and accomplishments are publicized to administrators who might not know the far-reaching concerns and effects of our LMC programs.

In addition to department publications, many schools also publish their own newsletters for their school communities.

ONLINE ACCESS

Information on the Department of Educational Media is available to the public at the DeKalb County School System's public website (http://www.dekalb.k12.ga.us/instruction/edmedia/). Here parents can find three grade-level suggested reading lists compiled by the DeKalb Teacher-Librarian

Advisory (DTLA) council. Teachers may access the LRC film booking site, Professional Library catalog, GALILEO (Georgia's virtual library), and more.

Similarly, the department offers an intranet site for use by employees within the system with information that includes handling of challenged materials, copyright issues, Georgia Performance Standards and accompanying lesson plans; position descriptions for LMSs, clerks, and long-term LMS substitutes; a photo directory of LMSs; instructional presentations; and various forms such as those for LMS evaluations. Useful hyperlinks, including one for the DeKalb Public Library, are also available there.

In addition to e-mail through the FirstClass system, LMSs have access to the *LMS Bulletin,* which communicates essential departmental information, and to conferencing through the LMS K–12 Office, which serves as a meeting place for LMSs to discuss issues of concern.

DEKALB TEACHER-LIBRARIAN ADVISORY COUNCIL

This group of eight LMSs, elected from among their peers, serves as an internal advocacy group promoting best practices. The council advises department personnel on professional issues, such as reviewing the prospective centralized catalog systems under consideration. It also responds to questions from LMSs on its LMS K12 electronic discussion list. The group advanced public relations in the community with three reading lists they compiled for elementary, middle, and high school students to assist parents with their children's reading. The DTLA council will serve as advisors to draft a new systemwide technology plan.

OBJECTIVES

Providing a path for good communication among LMSs offers creative ideas and problem solving to LMSs in their local schools. Administrators and the school community benefit from ready information on LMC programs and departmental expectations. One goal is to expand program offerings that promote diversity and inclusion throughout the school system. Good communication levels the playing field to ensure that each school and each LMS share information in the effort to offer their students the best.

SCHOOL LIBRARY MEDIA SPECIALIST'S LEADERSHIP ROLE

LMSs nominate and vote for members on the DTLA council. When evaluated after a year, the group was found useful by their colleagues who chose to continue it.

CONTRIBUTIONS TO STUDENT ACHIEVEMENT

By devising many paths of communication, public relations, and advocacy within and outside the system, we are increasing the avenues for our services to be known and understood. By informing the public, we give them ownership in our programs and thereby increase the likelihood of community support.

FUNDING

Our advocacy and public relations are funded through the local school district operating budget, with no additional funds required.

EVALUATION

Our FirstClass e-mail and conferencing system does not provide statistics. The system does allow monitoring, and the department benefits from the information revealed when comments provoke discussion to solve problems at the local schools.

Attracting and Keeping Parent Volunteers

DIANE H. THOMPSON
CHERRY CREEK HIGH SCHOOL, GREENWOOD VILLAGE, COLORADO

SUMMARY

Many, if not most, school libraries operate with fewer than optimal staff. Generally school libraries are fortunate to have one certified librarian and one support staff. Reliable parent volunteers are worth their weight in gold to help maintain a school library. At the Cherry Creek High School Library, a parent volunteer program has been in place for over twelve years.

Parents are invited to volunteer through the school newsletter and Parent-Teacher Community Organization meetings. Most volunteers return as long as they have a student attending high school. Before school begins, the librarian and a support staff person meet with the parent volunteer coordinator, who calls and schedules the new and returning volunteers. At the orientation meeting, new volunteers are given a tour of the Library Tech Center (LTC), meet all staff, and receive an invitation packet with a list of the volunteers, a volunteer ID, and a parking pass.

The library staff are committed to fulfilling parent volunteers' reasons for volunteering. Articles indicate volunteers want several things in exchange for their valuable time. First, they want to do work that is important to the library program. Our parents work at the circulation desk interacting with students, prepare books for addition to the collection, cover paperbacks with laminate, shelve books, pull books for displays, keep shelves in the correct order, help shift books as the collection grows, and help inventory the collection. We give them choices of tasks that need to be completed and try to fit the task to their preferences and skills.

Second, volunteers want to interact with other people and make social contact. They like to see the students and feel connected to their child's school. We make sure that volunteers have the opportunity to interact with students and staff.

Third, volunteers want to feel valued and appreciated. We always thank volunteers when they leave. A recent annual volunteer luncheon theme was "The Luck of the Irish." Our message was, "How lucky we are to have wonderful parent volunteers!" Each volunteer selects a new book to be dedicated to him or her for this service. A bookplate with the volunteer's name is added to the front page in the book they select. Each volunteer is also given a small appreciation gift.

Fourth, volunteers want to work in a pleasant atmosphere. All LTC staff know that an orderly, clean, spacious library provides the atmosphere that library users want. We each attend to any disarray, trash, or clutter that we see. At the end of every period, a general sweep is made of the facility. Students and staff working in the library are expected to use the facility in a manner that is respectful and courteous of others. Even when the library area is being used by over a hundred students, it is quiet and clean. Parent volunteers comment on what a pleasant facility the Cherry Creek High School Library is.

OBJECTIVE

The purpose of having regular parent volunteers in the library is to supplement paid support staffing. Parent volunteers do many tasks that help maintain the library collection in good condition.

SCHOOL LIBRARY MEDIA SPECIALIST'S LEADERSHIP ROLE

The teacher-librarian is responsible for the success of the volunteer program. She educates new staff members on the needs of volunteers and works closely with one support staff person to organize and oversee the program's function. Near the end of each school year, she and the support staff meet again with the parent volunteer coordinator to review the success of that year's program.

CONTRIBUTION TO STUDENT ACHIEVEMENT

The parent volunteer program contributes significantly to the ongoing improvement of the school library program by providing the skills and energy necessary to keep the library collection in good order, currency, and repair. Without their assistance, the library would be less appealing to students.

FUNDING

The library's supply budget funds materials for parent volunteers as well as expenses for making appreciation gifts, bookplates, and the cost of paper goods for the appreciation luncheon. Food for the luncheon is prepared and donated by all of the library staff. In addition to the benefits to the library of the additional help, the program generates a positive public image for the library.

Creating a Twenty-First-Century High School Library
MAGGIE SCHMUDE
NEW TRIER HIGH SCHOOL—WINNETKA CAMPUS, WINNETKA, ILLINOIS

SUMMARY

The New Trier Winnetka Campus Library had not been remodeled since 1957 and was no longer able to meet the needs of the school. In 2003, with the support of the school administration and board, a design team of twenty-five, consisting of the architect, the librarians and library support staff, representatives from five academic departments, the technology staff, and the physical plant services team, was convened under the leadership of the library department chair. (We also requested a student representative but were unable to find a student who wanted to attend 7:00 a.m. meetings!)

Prior to formation of the team, the architect spent several days with the library staff, observing them as they taught classes and watching what happened in the audiovisual and technical processing areas, as well as at the circulation desk, in order to see how we used space. We also conducted surveys with students and teachers to determine what they wanted in a new library. The needs of students and teachers were not parallel: students wanted access to a quiet study room, and teachers wanted spaces for their classes to meet.

Subcommittees identified the program needs for specific areas such as circulation and technical services. The architect completed many, many iterations of the drawings in designing a space that includes wireless networking, forty-four desktop computers and four wireless laptop carts, projection systems in each teaching space, an audiovisual facility with an audio booth and a green screen room that provides a pure color screen for filming so that backgrounds and special effects can be inserted during film editing; a peer tutoring/writing center, a quiet room, and separate areas that hold up to five classes simultaneously.

The remodeling took place over eight weeks in the summer of 2004. Planning for the remodeling was coordinated by the library department chair with the physical plant and technology staff. This team met weekly and created a calendar that indicated exactly what had to be done and when.

Intense collaboration among all stakeholders made this project unique and successful. The architect analyzed how we used space and designed accordingly, making changes as needed. Faculty and students made suggestions that were integrated into the final plan. Physical plant staff worked to make the move happen. Technology staff created network and computer use plans that complemented the way students currently use technology while providing for future growth and change.

OBJECTIVE

The major objective of the project was to create a usable, flexible space that served current needs and could be adapted for future needs.

SCHOOL LIBRARY MEDIA SPECIALIST'S LEADERSHIP ROLE

As chair of the design team, the library department chair was responsible for creating consensus among all the stakeholders in reaction to the work of the subcommittees that addressed particular areas.

CONTRIBUTION TO STUDENT ACHIEVEMENT

The remodeled space lends itself to different student learning styles and creates an excellent learning environment for both formal classes and individual student work.

FUNDING

The project was funded by the school board at just over $2 million.

EVALUATION

The effectiveness of this space is demonstrated by both an increase of 241 classes using the library from 2003 to 2004 and students' identifying the library as their first choice for technology use 62 percent of the time.

Audiovisual area, before
The former audiovisual area was dimly lit and did not provide a clear divide between storage and work space.

Audiovisual area, after
The new audiovisual area offers clearly defined storage space as well as brightly lit individual workstations.

Entrance area, before
Control gates and clutter
dominated the former hallway.

Entrance area, after
An arched ceiling, bright lights,
and offset carpeting provide a
clean and welcoming entrance
to the library.

Periodicals area, before
The lack of welcoming seating
in an ill-defined area limited
student use of periodicals.

Periodicals area, after
The new periodicals area provides comfortable seating for reading as well as study space for research in a clearly defined area with great natural light.

Study area, before
Lack of shelving space and too many study tables in a small space resulted in an unappealing study area.

Study area, after
An expanded study space with computers and natural lighting provides an attractive area for student use.

Doing the Best We Can with the Technology We Have

PATRICIA PICKARD
DEKALB COUNTY SCHOOL SYSTEM, DECATUR, GEORGIA

SUMMARY

In the DeKalb County School System, the Department of Educational Media is responsible for supporting the library programs in 131 schools and centers. Do we have all of the technology we want? No, not even close. Do we make the best use of the technology we have? We certainly try.

Demonstrating our commitment to support library technology, the Department of Educational Media employs one full-time library media specialist (LMS) with over twenty years of experience as a library technology specialist.

Our department collaborates with management information systems (MIS) to support a wide variety of technology in the library program:

- ➤ library media center use of the network
- ➤ installation, implementation, and support of the library automation application
- ➤ local school website design, instruction, and support
- ➤ an intranet site maintained by the Department of Educational Media
- ➤ installation, implementation, and support of school-selected reading and math applications

OBJECTIVES

In adopting a holistic approach to supporting library technology, our objectives are to

- ➤ allow instructional objectives to dictate how specific applications are installed and implemented
- ➤ provide library automation in-service sessions to all new LMSs as a group and ongoing help to all library media specialists individually both on-site and via remote viewing and control of the library media specialists' workstation
- ➤ streamline the distribution of the Online Public Access Catalog (OPAC) and reading/math applications to all workstations in each school building by using network utilities to distribute application files
- ➤ assist in offering beginning and advanced classes in school website design during the summer and twice during the school year to provide individual help as needed both on-site and via remote viewing and control of the LMSs workstation
- ➤ seek ways that various library applications can be used synergistically

By working collaboratively with MIS, the Department of Educational Media can provide library media specialists with well-functioning, dependable technology as well as the opportunities to develop the skills and confidence they need to set an example in their schools as leaders in the use of technology.

By demonstrating the use of technology as an administrative tool as well as a means of accessing and presenting information, they demonstrate to students and teachers that they are not only talking the talk but walking the walk. As they collaborate with teachers to use technology in learning activities, they are making the connection between efficient use of technology and student achievement.

SCHOOL LIBRARY MEDIA SPECIALIST'S LEADERSHIP ROLE

As instructional leaders in their individual schools, LMSs are in an excellent position to collaborate with the teachers and administrators to determine how applications can be installed and implemented to best meet the instructional needs of the school. It was the interest of the LMS in promoting school-selected reading and math applications that prompted the inclusion of these applications in the responsibilities of the library technology specialist.

The LMS's skill in conducting an effective reference interview was used to pinpoint exact symptoms and causes of technology problems and proved crucial in resolving these problems quickly. The technical know-how of LMSs contributed to their leadership role as they work with classroom teachers who may not have reached the same level of expertise. Working together, they are better able to plan units of study for students that integrate content, information literacy, and technology literacy objectives.

CONTRIBUTIONS TO STUDENT ACHIEVEMENT

Applications selected for their contribution to student achievement are overlapped for greater functionality:

We created a template that allows local schools to publish a searchable reading program quiz database on their local school websites. We export the quiz lists from the reading programs, import the data into an Access database, and post the database to the school website along with SQL (Structured Query Language) to query the database. By customizing the code for the font and color scheme, we are able to make the search and results page blend in with the rest of the local school's website.

Using a data conversion file purchased for use with the library automation program as a first step, we tweak student data records so that they can be imported into the reading and math applications. This time-saving function allows the LMS to introduce these applications to their faculties ready for them to use with their students.

Our intranet website is a comprehensive site providing information for, about, and by the LMSs. It includes the following information:

About Us
- ➤ Mission statement
- ➤ Professional standards and organizations
- ➤ Departmental policies
- ➤ Photo directory

Collection Development
- Review sources
- Bid vendors

Curriculum and Instruction
- Georgia performance standards
- Lesson plans and correlations
- Literacy checklists
- Technology Fair
- Reading Bowl

Resources
- Databases (state and district funding)
- Professional library online catalog
- PowerPoint presentations
- MARC records

Documents
- Forms
- Department memos
- Procedures and directions

FUNDING

Department of Educational Media funds, through the system's operating budget, purchase library automation software. Departmental funds paid for the library technology specialists to attend one week of network training, and the district funds her salary. Local schools and PTAs purchase reading and math applications.

EVALUATION

Prior to implementation:

- LMSs were unable to access all of the files or applications that they needed without going to other workstations or logging in as other users.
- Only workstations in the LMC had access to the OPAC.
- Few local schools had websites, and there were no searchable reading program quiz databases.
- Memos, forms, procedures, and policies were available in paper copies only; other information presented on the intranet site, such as the photo library directory (created by a local school library media specialist), was not available at all.
- The one-size-fits-all rule applied to installing and implementing reading and math applications purchased by the local schools.

The situation now:

➤ All LMSs are able to access the files and applications on the network that they need. They have access to all the files that library users save to the network, which gives the LMSs greater flexibility as they assist students with projects and portfolios. An additional drive mapping gives them direct and exclusive access to automation files on the server.

➤ We can push the OPAC and application updates to all workstations throughout the school buildings.

➤ A majority of the local schools have websites, and thirty-seven of them have searchable quiz databases. (See http://schools.dekalb.k12.ga.us/smokerise/library/search/ardefault.asp.)

➤ The department intranet site provides a wealth of information available in one comprehensive site.

➤ The local school's instructional objectives determine how the reading and math applications are installed and implemented. Decisions based on instruction and curriculum override technical convenience.

The Department of Educational Media's effective implementation of these technologies has also led to an attitude in which new technologies and the opportunity for improved applications are eagerly awaited.

Flexible Scheduling and Collaboration through FirstClass E-mail SySTEM

PATRICIA PICKARD
DEKALB COUNTY SCHOOL SYSTEM, DECATUR, GEORGIA

SUMMARY

To some in the DeKalb County School System, FirstClass is simply the county-provided e-mail program, but to library media specialists (LMSs), FirstClass is a tool for communication, scheduling, and collaboration. Scheduling classes, creating pathfinders, and contributing to systemwide discussion boards are just a few of the ways in which DeKalb school library media specialists maximize the use of FirstClass.

To assist with scheduling, many LMSs use FirstClass to maintain a virtual school LMC calendar that local school staff members can view from any Internet-connected computer. Teachers and administrators can easily see how the resources, spaces, and services of the LMC are being used. In addition to using the basic calendar, some LMSs assist teachers in seeing the relevance of specific activities to their programs by color-coding entries by grade level or the resources being used.

LMSs no longer need to send reminders of scheduled activities because the FirstClass calendar has the capacity to e-mail reminders directly to the teacher. Initial steps in collaboration can take place remotely through the availability of online request forms to schedule space or services. After the initial request form is submitted, the LMS can continue the collaboration virtually or face-to-face.

Each FirstClass account includes web space that several LMSs use to create virtual pathfinders for their patrons. Bookmarking important websites to guide students in finding the best Internet resources is as easy as directing them to print and nonprint resources located within the LMC itself. FirstClass provides a variety of templates for web pages within the program, so no additional software is necessary to create a professional-looking site of resources relevant to specific courses and assignments.

The Department of Educational Media maintains two conferences that all school library media specialists and media clerks have on their FirstClass desktops: LMS Bulletin and LMS K12 Conference. The LMS Bulletin is used for important announcements from the district department director and coordinators. The messages posted there pop up as each media specialist or clerk logs into FirstClass. This has replaced the need for paper memos sent through the county's courier system.

The LMS K12 Conference is used as a systemwide discussion board where LMSs post ideas and questions for one another. The discussion varies from day to day; it includes requests for specific copies of books, tips on capturing a screen shot, and many other needs. This is often the first place school library media specialists go with a question; they see it as the source of the collective knowledge of the district's school library media specialists. The needs of subgroups are supported through roundtables specifically developed for elementary, middle, high school, and other areas of interest.

While some of the district's departments do not use all tools available through FirstClass, LMSs use these tools to initiate learning, share ideas, and collaborate with teachers.

OBJECTIVES

The objective of the use of the FirstClass conferences and calendar was to increase communication within the local school and among LMCs. FirstClass meets this objective and also supports the district's goal to improve student achievement. It provides a way for teachers to communicate their information needs to the LMS quickly and easily so they can spend their time focusing on instruction in the classroom. In addition, LMC conferences in FirstClass give teachers access to pertinent instructional information with the click of a mouse.

SCHOOL LIBRARY MEDIA SPECIALIST'S LEADERSHIP ROLE

In each school, the LMS decides how the tools of FirstClass can best be used in the school library media program. Then the LMS customizes the resources for the needs of the school community. For example, an LMS might use a virtual calendar but not e-mail reminders for teachers for the color-coding of events.

The beginning of a new school year or new semester is an excellent time for implementation. At this time, an LMS can explain new procedures to teachers as well as ways to enhance resources. Also, an LMS can gradually add new aspects of FirstClass to the LMC's program and tweak them from year to year.

The best evaluation tool for LMSs is an increase in the use of facilities, resources, and space. As they try a new component of FirstClass, they can monitor usage statistics to see whether there is improvement.

CONTRIBUTIONS TO STUDENT ACHIEVEMENT

The use of FirstClass calendars and conferences helps to increase the visibility and effectiveness of the library media program in each school. It gives the LMS one more way to extend programs outside the LMC itself. This additional communication and collaboration supports resource-based teaching and increased student achievement. As LMSs continue to explore the many capabilities of FirstClass, the result will be continued growth and development to meet the needs of the school communities.

FUNDING

There is no special funding for the LMSs to implement this communication tool. The school system provides FirstClass e-mail access to all certificated and classified employees. Funding comes from the system operating budget.

EVALUATION

When surveyed on the LMS K12 Conference how they were using FirstClass, most of the media specialists who responded said that the virtual calendar for scheduling has been very successful. Although it is more preparation work for the LMS to set up the calendars, providing teachers with a calendar that can be checked from their desks or home has been a valuable resource.

Strengthening the Library Media Program

DONNA HELVERING
MILLARD PUBLIC SCHOOLS, OMAHA, NEBRASKA

The Millard Public Schools, successful campaign to double the library budget during a time of budget cuts and increasing enrollments illustrates many of the principles of effective budget development. The objective of this campaign was to provide world-class resources for students and staff.

This campaign's success resulted from multiple factors. First, the school library media staff recognized that access to online databases was an increasingly important aspect of a quality school library media program. Before the campaign, each school was required to pay for databases from its local budgets, leading to uneven access to information. The campaign focused on the cost savings and increased quality that could result from pooling these resources. Involving students and staff from across the district in database trials resulted in wide support for this program, as all members of the community realized the potential impact of increased database access on student achievement.

The campaign also integrated the communication of data at the local level. Monthly newsletters from the school library media specialists included information on use of the collection, number of drop-in visits, and number of scheduled classes. The role of the school library media specialist as an instructional leader was demonstrated by a listing of participation in school and district committees and mentoring of clubs for students. The impact on individual assignments of each school library media center was shown by describing the resources used in individual curriculum units in which the school library media specialist had been a collaborative partner.

As a result of the use of these strategies, the district budget was increased by $100,000. Discounts that were provided by group purchase of databases allowed the district to add fifteen new age-appropriate resources for all 20,000 students. The increased number of databases and the involvement of students and staff in database trials led to an 80 percent increase in home access to databases. The availability of additional resources and a greater awareness of the value of integrated curriculum units have contributed to substantial increases in test scores for fourth- and eighth-grade language arts.

Library Programming

ANNE O'MALLEY
NEW TRIER HIGH SCHOOL—NORTHFIELD CAMPUS, NORTHFIELD, ILLINOIS

SUMMARY

The New Trier High School District has two schools: the Northfield Campus provides a transition from middle school to the Winnetka Campus for sophomores, juniors, and seniors. Since the opening of the freshman campus in 2001, New Trier librarians have sought to establish programming and other activities for freshman students and staff. Our central mission is to work with teachers to integrate research and outside reading into the curriculum, and we also wanted to shape our library's image as a place to come for nonclass activities. We accomplish this goal by celebrating Teen Read Week and National Library Week; implementing our state's new high school reading promotion, the Abe Lincoln Readers' Choice Award; and strategizing new promotions and other projects. Some of our activities are

- ➤ Math help sessions prior to math semester exams. This half-day session is led by a library staff member (a former math teacher), two Academic Assistance Center staffers, and an array of volunteer math teachers.
- ➤ Holiday and winter story reading just before winter break, read by library staff administrators and other volunteers. Readers sign up a few weeks before the event. They choose their favorite story or ask for suggestions. Several teachers bring their classes to listen.
- ➤ Author visits, including author alumni. New Trier has an active educational foundation that connects with alumni and gathers their information of interest to the school. We will try to find an audience for any published author who is willing to make a visit.
- ➤ Poetry performances celebrating Black History Month. We have a staff member who is a specialist in poetry of African American authors. We invite theater classes and anyone else who is interested to enjoy three performances each year.
- ➤ "Lunch and Learns" to promote new materials, databases, or other information. We have introduced new databases, shown catalog tips, and highlighted new titles of interest to

departments. We have presented for all staff on topics such as Google tips and offered preview sessions for upcoming school events, including opera visits and a special day honoring Chinese culture and performing arts.

➤ Bring the voting to them. We were concerned that not enough students would vote in the Abe Lincoln Readers' Choice Award program even though we had promoted the contest all year, and so we decided to bring the voting to the cafeteria for lunch periods. It was easy to connect with readers there, and we had little doubt that offering voting in the cafeteria increased participation.

➤ Ikebana and haiku too. April is National Poetry Month, and we were looking for a change from our poetry contests of the past few years. We approached our Japanese teacher, who was happy to work on a unit on haiku that involved a library presentation and also to move her flower arranging lesson to the library, where the completed projects were displayed. We hung illustrated haiku that the students composed, interspersed them with the flower arrangements, and had a special viewing day with Japanese tea and other treats.

OBJECTIVES

Our main objective is to make sure that the library is viewed as a student- and staff-friendly operation. We want to maintain a welcoming environment and be a creative, proactive source of programming to benefit the whole school.

SCHOOL LIBRARY MEDIA SPECIALIST'S LEADERSHIP ROLE

We plan all the programs, collaborating with departments, and are more than happy to collaborate when teachers come to us. These teacher initiatives include special collaborations for National Library Week and a day devoted to Trev Expo, a science fair that uses the library not just for research but for activity space on the day of the event.

CONTRIBUTIONS TO STUDENT ACHIEVEMENT

Our activities, promotions, and programming foster a positive public image for our library. We believe that when the library is an active, popular resource for the whole school, it shows that libraries are necessary. As we initiate and continue successful programs, our repertoire expands, our reputation grows in the school community, and we secure our library's important role in the life of the school.

FUNDING

Our library budget covers funding for food, contest prizes, and display supplies. We have not yet needed to pay outside speaker fees or invest in costly equipment. Should a more expensive project be on the horizon, we would investigate the possibility of grants or other funding resources.

EVALUATION

We evaluate informally and assess whether to repeat a particular activity. Sometimes quantitative data work. Well over 10 percent of students voted in the Readers' Choice Award program in 2005;

this is considered successful given that participation demanded outside-of-class reading for our busy students. But class participation was down a little for holiday readings the past year. We will determine the reasons for this decline as we consider programs for next year. Much of our evaluation takes place in informal discussions based on input from students and staff.

Mentoring School Library Media Specialists New to the System

PATRICIA PICKARD
DEKALB COUNTY SCHOOL SYSTEM, DECATUR, GEORGIA

SUMMARY

The philosophy and practice of providing support and mentoring to library media specialists (LMSs) new to the DeKalb County School System is a priority in the Department of Educational Media. Meaningful program activities are planned and delivered to LMSs in an organized manner through ongoing programs, events, and personnel support:

Orientation: A content-specific orientation for LMSs new to the system is provided by the department. Attendees are divided by level of assignment: elementary (morning) and middle and high school (afternoon). During this time, the director and coordinators share departmental objectives and services provided to support the LMSs and their programs.

Mentoring program: A mentoring program framework is provided for all new LMSs, pairing each with a mentor who works at the same program level. Mentors are asked to participate in the program based on their experience, program-level assignment, and willingness to offer their support to newcomers. A luncheon is provided for the mentors and mentees on the day of the orientation. Mentors and mentees are introduced to each other, information about the program is presented, and the responsibilities of the mentors and mentees are discussed.

Librarian-at-large: Although a mentoring program is in place that encourages peer-to-peer school-level support, the Department of Educational Media saw the need to add system-level support. The librarian-at-large position was added in 2000 in expansion of the LMS's job description and the need to provide professional support in schools that were without an LMS. The librarian at-large is the official mentor to all new LMSs, and in this role she supports and trains new LMSs, provides local on-site school support, and coordinates the New Teacher–Librarian Class series. In addition, the librarian-at-large assists when a school must hire a long-term substitute, working with the substitute and clerk to keep the library program functioning in the LMS's absence.

New Teacher–Librarian Class: The librarian-at-large coordinates a series of classes offered during the fall semester for new LMSs. Class sessions include system policies and procedures, suggested program activities, reading initiatives, Spectrum automated library system training, Georgia Media Specialist Evaluation Instrument, resources from the Professional Library, Fernback Science Center, learning resources center, GALILEO (Georgia's state virtual library), professional organizations, and GAMA (the student library organization). One professional learning unit is awarded for completion of the series of classes.

OBJECTIVES

This program supports the school and district goals of providing orientation and training for new staff by providing a content-specific program for LMSs, establishing a support network for them, and developing a peer mentoring program to support new LMSs. This program acclimates staff to the district as well as to the specific school or department setting. Our success in meeting these objectives determines the effectiveness of the library program and our impact on student learning and achievement.

SCHOOL LIBRARY MEDIA SPECIALIST'S LEADERSHIP ROLE

The Department of Educational Media plans, implements, and evaluates this program through debriefing sessions held in the department following program activities. Changes are made based on evaluative data provided by the new LMSs, program presenters, and members of the department.

CONTRIBUTIONS TO STUDENT ACHIEVEMENT

The mentoring and support program activities guide LMSs new to DeKalb as they develop their own unique and pivotal role within their schools. When LMSs are grounded in their knowledge and acclimated to district, department, and school expectations, they are better able to assist students in becoming effective users of information. These activities are also developed to address issues of retention of the LMSs who are successful in their practice.

FUNDING

The mentoring and support efforts described are funded through the local school district budget with no additional funds required.

EVALUATION

This mentoring program is evaluated in multiple ways:

- ➤ LMS evaluation forms of the program and activities are used to monitor the opinions of the new LMSs and determine the overall usefulness of the classes to new teacher-librarians.
- ➤ The participation rate of new LMSs is evaluated, as well as reasons for not attending a session or program activity.
- ➤ The Department of Educational Media has debriefing sessions to review activities and make needed changes in program offerings.

Partnerships: School and Public Libraries

MARY TRENERRY, STEPHANIE BEISCH
MILLARD PUBLIC SCHOOLS, MILLARD SOUTH HIGH SCHOOL, OMAHA, NEBRASKA

SUMMARY

Our collaborations began several years ago when Millard Branch young adult librarian Paul Christopherson asked us to distribute pamphlets to our high school students promoting the summer reading program at the Millard Branch of the Omaha Public Library. The following activities have developed because of that first small step:

➤ Paul comes to our district monthly meetings. He relates news from the public library, learns the latest happenings in our schools, and shares a young adult book.

➤ We have collaborated and presented a session at the Nebraska Library Association and Nebraska Educational Media Association Joint Conference telling other librarians about our efforts.

➤ When Paul needed speakers for a citywide teen art project to talk about Omaha and library history, he asked media specialists from Millard Public Schools to participate, and we did so gladly.

➤ We schedule a day in May for Paul to visit our school to give booktalks and tell students about the programs the public library will offer for teens in the summer. The participation in the teen programs has more than doubled since he started visiting.

➤ When our high school students need volunteer hours, we contact Paul, who arranges for students to meet with the volunteer coordinator at the public library.

➤ Millard South High School has a unique school-within-a-school for at-risk students. We have asked Paul to present booktalks for these students and encourage them to attend young adult programs offered at the public library.

➤ Paul spearheaded an effort to get library cards for teachers who live outside but teach inside the public library boundaries. This enables these teachers to get materials to use in their classrooms. We promote this benefit to staff.

➤ We alert Paul when big projects are assigned in any subject area, and he works to get more materials at the Millard Branch to assist our students.

From a simple start of handing out pamphlets, there are now many Millard Public School media specialists who work collaboratively with our public library on a variety of projects.

OBJECTIVE

Our objective is to make our students aware of the variety of resources available to them at the public library. This supports two key parts of our district's mission statement that encourage "(1) a partnership of students, home, school and community, and (2) broad-based and diverse educational opportunities."

CONTRIBUTION TO STUDENT ACHIEVEMENT

Our coordinated efforts introduce young adults to the dynamics of the public library with all its resources, which greatly promote lifelong learning.

SCHOOL LIBRARY MEDIA SPECIALIST'S LEADERSHIP ROLE

We have embraced the opportunities that the public library provides for students by our encouragement, promotion, and participation. In addition to announcements at school, we post fliers, write articles for the parent newsletter, e-mail staff, and present information at faculty meetings.

FUNDING

All of our collaboration activities fall under our regular duties; no extra funds were needed.

EVALUATION

We receive ongoing feedback from our students, staff, and public library. All have had positive comments. Paul has shared statistics that indicate participation in the young adult summer program has more than doubled since our collaboration began years ago, as well as a substantial increase in the teen volunteer program.

Educating Parents about the School Library Subscription Databases

KRISTIN MCKEOWN
CHERRY CREEK HIGH SCHOOL, GREENWOOD VILLAGE, COLORADO

SUMMARY

Few things disturb a librarian more than the idea of library resources that are being underused. It is from this spirit of maximizing library use that the idea for the database presentation was born.

It began on Cherry Creek High School's annual back-to-school night. As parents were rapidly making their way through their teenagers' schedules, attending ten-minute "classes" with teachers, and then racing off to the next class, they had brief pockets of time during off-periods that they spent in the library. Since our time with parents was so short, the team decided to focus on one area: showing parents the resources that students can access from home. Every parent we spoke with was unfamiliar with the library's online subscription databases, and all were impressed by the richness of these resources.

As we reflected on the parents' enthusiastic responses, the teacher-librarian team realized this was a rich advocacy and public relations opportunity. We determined that the best venue for educating parents is our school's monthly Parent-Teacher Community Organization (PTCO) meeting.

After contacting the PTCO president and arranging a time, two of the teacher-librarians began preparing for the presentation. Because we realized that few parents at the meeting would be prepared with pen and paper, we assembled a small packet of handouts with our home access card attached, a guide to some of our general periodical and content-specific databases, a handout entitled "What's Wrong with Googling?" and a packet outlining how to create an account in and effectively use our subscription citation maker, NoodleBib.

The greatest challenge was to draft a presentation that touched on the value of these resources and demonstrated the basics of accessing them without taking too much time. We decided to summarize the message of our "What's Wrong with Googling?" handout as succinctly as possible, spending most of our time demonstrating what these databases can do. We broke the demonstration into two sections: general periodical indexes and content-specific databases. For the general periodical indexes, we used EBSCOhost to locate an article that the researcher already knew of or had heard about. Then we quickly showed the various social issues databases available: SIRS, Thomson Gale's Opposing Viewpoints, and FACTS.com's Issues and Controversies.

For the content-specific databases, we reviewed the features of the ABC-CLIO social studies databases, focusing on the breadth of information and each article's active interconnectedness to other related articles through links. At this point in the presentation, our time was running short, so after pointing out where parents and students could find information relating to literature and literacy criticism, we moved on to the final segment of our presentation: NoodleBib.

The teacher-librarians are enthusiastic proponents of the citation tool NoodleBib, but some faculty members have been reluctant to use a citation maker for fear of denying students the experience of constructing bibliographic citations "the old-fashioned way." With the expectation that some parents may agree with this perspective, we emphasized during our presentation that NoodleBib is a teaching tool students can use at home without the presence of an expert in the MLA (Modern Language Association) format. The parent response was very positive.

While the presentation was a success, it will take more than one meeting to make certain that most, if not all, parents know about the library's databases. Our plan is to expand this presentation, sharing more information about online resources with parents in several shorter presentations over the course of a school year. The frequency of a library presence at parent meetings like these gives the library program a meaningful visibility beyond our work with students and teachers. It is this visibility that will reinforce in their minds that the library and its resources are here for their children as well as for them.

OBJECTIVES

The goals of this practice are to maximize the use of library resources and support student achievement. By familiarizing parents with the library's subscription databases, the teacher-librarian creates allies in our mission to foster excellence in research. This directly supports our school and district's goals of creating lifelong learners and successful users of information.

SCHOOL LIBRARY MEDIA SPECIALIST'S LEADERSHIP ROLE

Two members of the teacher-librarian team planned and implemented the PTCO presentation. As a result of the time constraints, we determined which information was essential and then included the appropriate supplementary materials in the parent folders. We videotaped the presentation so that we could better evaluate the experience and make necessary improvements for the next presentation. We also solicited feedback from the PTCO president regarding her assessment of the presentation's success.

CONTRIBUTIONS TO STUDENT ACHIEVEMENT

School libraries are no longer mere brick-and-mortar structures open to students only during the school day. With remote access, library resources are available twenty-four hours a day from any place that has an Internet connection. With this increased flexibility comes a need not only to teach students the skills they need to independently research but also to recruit parents to reinforce this process. Familiarizing parents with the electronic resources available is one component of forging this alliance. The Cherry Creek High School community prides itself on its parent involvement and support of student achievement; this partnership between the library program and parent community is another extension of this kind of involvement.

FUNDING

The planning for this presentation took place between the teacher-librarians during the school day. Other than the agenda handout, most of the materials handed out during the presentation had been previously created for student instruction. The only cost was for additional copies and the folders handed out to parents.

EVALUATION

By videotaping the presentation, we were able to look back at what elements were clear or unclear, appropriately or inappropriately timed, and so forth. We also sought feedback from the PTCO president. For future presentations, we would like to touch base with parents at a following PTCO meeting or perhaps ask parents to complete a brief feedback form to be shared with the teacher-librarian. We could also analyze the database home use statistics when available.

School and Public Library Collaboration

PATRICIA PICKARD
DEKALB COUNTY SCHOOL SYSTEM, DECATUR, GEORGIA

SUMMARY

Students and teachers are winners when school and public library professionals work together to support reading promotion programs, provide informational programs, assist patrons in K–12 schools, address information literacy standards and skills; and offer basic access to computer technology. The following are examples of collaboration that occur between the DeKalb County School System and the DeKalb County Public Library System:

Sharing expertise of staff members: The exchange of presenters for library-related professional learning activities is a growing practice in our school and public library system. A recent speaker exchange involved a reading specialist presenting "How Children Learn to Read" to public librarians and two public librarians presenting "Getting Graphic: Learning about Graphic Novels" to school library media personnel.

Collaborating on publications: A team of library media specialists (LMSs), teachers, and public librarians worked together to develop a K–12 summer reading list for students. Distribution sites included schools, public libraries, bookstores, summer recreational facilities, and availability using the DeKalb County School System website.

Programming for high school students: Public librarians develop and host programs targeting the interests of middle school and high school students. Sample programs include "The College Fair," "Poetry Jam," and "Master Shakespeare and the Craft of Acting." In the spring, the school and public librarians collaboratively plan programs to encourage student reading with summer reading programs. When school reopens in the fall, many LMSs recognize students who participated in the public library program as a way to provide an incentive to students who are traditionally nonreaders.

Sharing a quarterly newsletter: Public librarians produce a quarterly newsletter of electronic resources, *E-Resource News,* and e-mail the publication to LMSs. In turn, LMSs share the publication, which highlights databases, websites, and recent books, with teachers and students.

Georgia Peach Book Award program school: LMSs and public librarians collaborated to establish the Georgia Peach Book Award program for high school students. Modeled after a local grassroots "battle of the books" competition entitled the Helen Ruffin Reading Bowl, books of interest to teenagers are selected. Benefits of the competition include improved reading comprehension, awareness of the diversity of genres, creation of team spirit and cooperation, and heightened awareness of leisure reading among high school students.

Electronic school assignment alert form: Communication between LMSs and public librarians about students' research assignments is critical to ensure resources and availability of assistance from the library staff when students visit the public library. Contacts are made between school and public library professionals by telephone calls, faxes, or the electronic school assignment alert form.

DeKalb R.E.A.D.S. book character: Students in the school system participate in a variety of reading incentive programs and have access to print and electronic resources. To summarize the various resources and reading programs, the Department of Educational Media collaborated with a graphic artist and computer graphic artist to create the "DeKalb R.E.A.D.S." character. The character is available as a poster and screen saver for computer monitors.

OBJECTIVES

The objectives of the school and public library collaboration are to

- ➤ introduce students and teachers to resources that promote literacy
- ➤ provide resources and programs to address academic assignments and personal interests
- ➤ show the seamless transition of using resources at the school and public libraries

SCHOOL LIBRARY MEDIA SPECIALIST'S LEADERSHIP ROLE

As the primary contact person between the school and public library, the LMS collaborates with public librarians in a leadership role to plan and implement special programs. These programs emphasize the joys of reading and literacy, facilitate the sharing of information related to students' research assignments, and establish interlibrary loan privileges as needed. Formal and informal evaluation strategies are available and employed for monitoring the number of students participating in special programs and interviewing students about their experiences in using the school and public libraries.

CONTRIBUTIONS TO STUDENT ACHIEVEMENT

Representatives from the DeKalb County School System and the DeKalb County Public Library System provide leadership for a local task force, "Job Alike," which focuses on the commonalities between the two library organizations. These include print and electronic resources; availability of electronic resources twenty-four hours a day, Monday through Saturday, using the Internet; age-appropriate programs in school and public libraries; and expertise from library personnel in supporting student achievement and lifelong learning. The availability of information and involvement of personnel support the mission statements of the school and public library systems.

Our collaboration with public librarians is unique because of the frequency of communication with library colleagues. At the annual meeting of school library personnel at the beginning of the school year, representatives of the public library share information about services and programs available to school communities. Exchange of contact information between school and public library professionals is common practice. Public librarians serve as members of the local school library media/technology committee, which serves as an advisory and advocacy group for the library media program. During professional learning miniconferences, the school system sponsored public librarians to conduct concurrent sessions on topics that support literacy and collection development.

FUNDING

Generally the programs for students, teachers, and library personnel occur during operational hours of the school and public libraries, creating no additional costs for personnel and resources. Print and electronic resources and supplies are provided through the general funding available to each organization, with the exception of GALILEO, the statewide virtual library funded by the Georgia legislature.

EVALUATION

Evaluation of the collaborative relationship between the school and public libraries is qualitative and quantitative. LMSs report the involvement of public librarians in school activities such as Library Card Sign-up Month, Children's Books Week, and Black History Month; membership on the school library media/technology committee; and visits to promote the vacation reading program. Participation by public librarians increases each year, and reports from the LMSs reflect greater collegiality and appreciation for the collaboration.

In the fall of 2005, one LMS reported a 459 percent increase in student participation in the summer reading program. Laurie Crooks, LMS at Stone Mountain Elementary School, responded to the question, "What do you think caused this large increase in student participation?"

> At the end of last school year, I plastered posters everywhere, talked about the programs, offered prizes, passed out bookmarks, and sent home information about signing up at the public library. Mid-first semester of this year we sent out invitations to a congratulatory "tea" to the public library Summer Reading participants. The public librarian came with freebies from the program, our AP [assistant principal] contributed some gift items, the Reading Specialist brought paperback books, and a vendor representative provided posters. Everybody got something when his/her name was pulled from a basket. We had cake, cookies, and drinks, a reward for their summer reading, but also for actually signing up and going to the library. I think that [the increase] was because we enthusiastically pushed it at every session in the media center from the time the program was announced to us.

Transition from a Fixed Schedule to a Flexible Schedule in an Elementary School

JANIE KOSSAK
AUSTIN ELEMENTARY SCHOOL, DEKALB COUNTY SCHOOL SYSTEM,
DUNWOODY, GEORGIA

SUMMARY

Flexible schedule is defined as a "library media center schedule that is arranged by the library media specialist in consultation with classroom teachers."[17] Flexible scheduling contrasts with fixed scheduling in which classes are assigned specific times for library use with no consideration of collaborative planning time for library media specialists and teachers. Implementing flexible access to an elementary library media program's space, resources, and services is best practice. And it is also very hard! The key to implementing this enormous change is to remember that the process does not start with implementation. First comes initiation, then implementation, and finally continuation.

Initiation is the process leading up to the decision to make the change. This process can begin as part of your interview for a new library media specialist (LMS) position. When the principal asks if you have any questions, say, "Yes!" and start asking. "Do students currently have flexible access to the library media program's space, resources, and services?" If the answer is not a resounding "yes, they do," then it is time to begin educating your prospective new principal on the benefits of this best practice. Have ready copies of research studies that support flexible access. By doing this, you have begun to earn your principal's respect as an LMS who puts student achievement first and knows the best way to administer an effective library program.

When presenting information to faculty and staff during a meeting, showcase your teaching skills by being more than a talking head and model instructional design principles in your presentation. Once the principal understands flexible access and is willing to support it (this normally does not happen overnight), you can begin to educate the media committee on flexible access as best practice. Rather than being the only change agent, encourage media committee members to take lead roles in creating the proposal that will be presented to faculty and staff. Focus all discussion on student achievement to prevent a tug-of-war between teachers who may be faced with less planning time when library classes are not scheduled and flexible access is used instead.

During the implementation phase, the change to flexible scheduling will be put into practice. Again work with the media committee to establish policies and procedures to support flexible access. As often as possible, demonstrate your service orientation by putting people before paper or computer work. Invite collaboration with teachers rather than waiting for a teacher to ask for your help. Remember that they have been working with an LMS who was busy teaching classes all day and did not have time to help someone else teach a lesson. And above all, recognize that some people are reluctant to change because of fear of the unknown.

Finally, acceptance of the change as a sustained part of practice or the continuation phase will begin. Take a moment to reflect on the journey; congratulate your principal, your staff, and yourself for making the change to flexible scheduling; and then get back to work. Survey teachers and students to make sure that the space, resources, and services are adequate. Gather and report statistics. Offer your assistance whenever and wherever you can. And above all, enjoy managing a dynamic, busy heart of the school library media center.

OBJECTIVE

The objective of this best practice is to provide students with increased access to the library and information, specifically at their point of need. The DeKalb County School System board policy endorses students' flexible access to the library media center during each school day.

SCHOOL LIBRARY MEDIA SPECIALIST'S LEADERSHIP ROLE

The LMS is the initial change agent. It is her responsibility to know the research that supports flexible access and be able to communicate the benefits to the school community. Once the LMS presents flexible access as supported by research as a best practice strategy and educates the faculty and staff on its benefits, her role is one of advisor and facilitator. Above all, the LMS's role is to maintain the focus on student achievement.

CONTRIBUTIONS TO STUDENT ACHIEVEMENT

With flexible access, students have immediate, anytime access to information in our library media center. With teacher permission or that of parents during after-school time, they are allowed to come daily to the media center whenever they have a need or desire for information. The LMS regularly collaborates with teachers, and information skills are taught through core subjects rather than in isolation.

FUNDING

The activities to move toward flexible scheduling occur during the school day and are accommodated within current funding for staff provided by each school.

EVALUATION

This best practice is evaluated annually through student and teacher surveys, statistics provided through the automated circulation system, and student achievement on standardized tests.

NOTES

1. Steven Baule, "Success with Budget Proposals," in *School Library Management,* 5th ed., edited by Catherine Andronik (Worthington, OH: Linworth Publishing, 2003), 169.
2. Diane Oberg, "School Libraries: Inviting Spaces for Learning," in *The Whole School Library Handbook,* edited by Blanche Woolls and David V. Loertscher (Chicago: American Library Association, 2005), 196.
3. Joan Frye Williams, "Making Sense of the Future" (presentation at the 2006 *School Library Journal* Summit, Chicago, November 4, 2006), retrieved February 3, 2008, from http://extras.schoollibraryjournal.com/summit/2006/presentations.html.
4. Rolf Erikson and Carolyn Markuson, *Designing a School Library Media Center for the Future* (Chicago: American Library Association, 2001), 23–24.
5. Douglas L. Zweizig, "Access and Use of Library Resources in Library Power," *School Libraries Worldwide* 5, no. 2 (1999): 22.
6. Marla McGhee and Barbara A. Jansen, *The Principal's Guide to a Powerful Library Media Program* (Worthington, OH: Linworth Publishing, 2005), 122–123.
7. Donna Helvering, "Sustaining the Program," Statement on Best Practices submitted as ancillary material for this volume, 2006.
8. Keith Curry Lance, Marcia J. Rodney, and Christien Hamilton-Pennel, "Powerful Libraries Make Powerful Learners: The Illinois Study" (Canton: Illinois School Library Media Association, 2005), 2.
9. Zweizig, "Access and Use of Library Resources in Library Power," 16.
10. Ibid., 19.
11. Ibid., 20.
12. Jo Ann Brandi, "Power Up Performance: Nine Ways to Keep Employees Engaged," accessed April 19, 2007, at http://www.hr.com.
13. Gary Hartzell, "The Whole Truth: Librarians Need to Emphasize What They Have to Offer," in *The Whole School Library Handbook,* ed. Woolls and Loertscher, 287.
14. Steven M. Baule and Laura Blair Bertani, "How to Gain Support from Your Board and Administration," in *The Whole School Library Handbook,* ed. Woolls and Loertscher, 295–297.
15. "Every Student Succeeds @ your library: Strategic Marketing for School Library Media Centers; Participant Manual Facilitator Guide" (Chicago: American Library Association/American Association of School Librarians, 3M Systems, April 2003), 9.
16. Retrieved from the American Association of School Librarians website: http://www.ala.org/ala/aasl/aaslproftools/informationpower/informationpower.cfm.
17. American Association for School Librarians, *A Planning Guide for Information Power Building Partnerships for Learning* (Chicago: American Association of School Librarians, 1999), p. 42.

CHAPTER 5

Creating a Vision for the Future of School Library Media Programs

Creating a vision for the future of library media programs requires the integration of technology in teaching and learning, a commitment to reflection and continuous assessment, long-range planning that supports the school library media specialist's role as instructional partner and school leader, and involvement in building the educational environment of the future.

Technology as a resource not only for information access but for information communication and production of new information is an essential part of the vision of school library media programs in creating a "vibrant learning community."[1] Technology has played a prominent role in guidelines for school library media centers since 1975.[2] However, the requirements of No Child Left Behind for technology literacy, the International Society for Technology in Education's development of technology standards for all members of the education community, and the results of school library impact studies on the contributions of strong technology environments on student achievement will propel the integration of technology more fully into the school library media center. (See http://www.lrs.org.)

This integration of technology into teaching and learning and as a critical role of the school library media program serves as the basis for many guidelines for student learning.[3] This integration of information and technology literacy with the content areas is also a hallmark of the Partnership for 21st Century Skills ICT Literacy Maps (http://www.21stcenturyskills.org/index.php?option=com_content&task=view&id=31&Itemid=33%20), which provide a structure for collaboration that supports the work of the library media specialist as a collaboration leader.

The integration of technology into teaching and learning can also address the digital divide. Access provided by many of the NSLMPY programs to the school library media center before and after school hours meets the needs of students who do not have computers and electronic resources in their home environment. In addition, the multiple formats available through technology allow the school to respond to the needs of students who do not learn from traditional text resources or whose learning preferences have been shaped by a lifetime in an environment rife with visual images and auditory stimulation. A highlight of the 2005 site visits by the NSLMPY committee was the opportunity to observe the teaching of a multimedia unit at Downer's Grove South High School (Illinois). In this unit, the social studies teacher and the library media specialist worked with students as they created music videos illustrative of specific periods in history. In compiling these videos, the students used print resources and databases but also carefully selected visual images that illustrated the lyrics of a specific protest song. The students then produced music videos using print, visual, audio, and multimedia resources. The students' discussion of these videos, held informally and confidentially with NSLMPY committee members, did not focus on the software and equipment used to produce these videos. Rather, the students discussed how these new information resources illustrated and reflected the social context in which these protest songs were written.

Advances in technology equipment and resources may assist school library media centers in integrating technology into their support of teaching and learning. The availability of wireless computing and mobile laptop labs can reduce the space demands of a desktop computer lab. Wireless computing and mobile labs can be taken to learners in their environment and extend the reach and impact of the school library media program. Web 2.0 technologies can provide access to information in multiple formats (e.g., Flickr and Google Maps) as well as to resources for creating new sources of information (e.g., Backpack and Whiteboard). (See http://www.go2web20.net for a listing of Web 2.0 applications.)

Because the work of effective school library media specialists intersects with all areas of the school, it is imperative that they be on the school's technology team. Their knowledge of the curriculum, specific assignments, electronic resources, and technology can assist in developing a technology environment centered on student learning.

In this book's closing vignettes, Patricia Pickard takes us "into the future" with her description of the results of assessment and long-range planning on the success of the DeKalb County, Georgia, School District. An additional perspective on the value of assessment is provided by Katherine Lowe. A vision of the future of education guided Carolyn Kirio and the Kapolei community in designing a new high school.

About the Future

PATRICIA PICKARD
DEKALB COUNTY SCHOOL SYSTEM, DECATUR, GEORGIA

SUMMARY

Vision connotes wisdom to plan for the future. In the DeKalb County School System, our library programs and library management have evolved over the existence of the Department of Educational Media now more than thirty years old. Our vision for student achievement in the next generation has initiated changes at the system level.

Unique positions in the Department of Educational Media support the essential priority work of library media specialists (LMSs) in the schools:

Acquisitions secretary: LMSs are relieved of the paperwork tasks of placing book orders and paying invoices. A departmental acquisitions secretary serves as their bookkeeper, so collaboration and teaching are the first priority of the schoolhouse. This setting of priorities is essential to student achievement, the bottom line for the district.

District professional librarian: This librarian serves employees of DeKalb with the Professional Library's print collection, online resources, interlibrary loan, grant information, and more. Subscriptions to professional journals and circulation to teachers in the schools protect local school budgets for student need. Our professional librarian teaches local faculties about services and resources available to them at the system level. This position is held by a highly qualified librarian with school and public library management experience.

Technology librarian: As library systems became increasingly sophisticated, a position was established to support and maintain our servers supporting automated circulation and catalog systems in each of our 131 schools. The technology librarian serves as a liaison with our school system's management information systems (MIS) department. This position is held by a highly qualified former LMS with high-level technology skills and talent.

Librarian-at-large: This position was added in 2000 as a mentoring position for new LMSs. With the expansion of the LMS's position description and LMSs coming from a variety of backgrounds, this position is essential to a first-year LMS's survival. In addition, our at-large librarian serves to assist when a school must hire a long-term substitute, working with the clerk to keep the library program functioning in the absence of the LMS. This position is held by a highly experienced, award-winning former LMS.

THEMES

A motivational theme is adopted each year by the director of the department to provide direction and focus for our library media specialists. For the past several years, the primary theme, Visibility and Effectiveness, has carried a subtheme, which changes each year. In 2004, for example, the subtheme was Fostering Higher Expectations for Teacher-Librarians. Recent themes have focused on use of the title "teacher-librarians" and creating a culture of reading, under the umbrella of Visibility and Effectiveness. Using this theme in our publications reminds not only LMSs but also administrators and others in our school communities of the expectations we have for ourselves and our programs.

AUTOMATION SUPPORT

Our school libraries have had automated circulation and catalog systems for many years, first with Winnebago and now Sagebrush Spectrum. We are fortunate to have a technology librarian who works exclusively with LMSs to support and maintain the 131 servers required and answer questions about complex software functions. We are now planning for the future with a centralized catalog as a major piece of the plan. The technology librarian will oversee this process, maintaining 1 server instead of 131. We are uniquely prepared to move forward with this, since the Department of Educational Media employs a professional cataloging department with membership in the Southeastern Library Network, the sole source for Online Computer Library Center cataloging in the Southeast. Catalogers will make professional cataloging decisions for the new centralized system.

Our vision for the future involves not only the dream of a centralized catalog but also freeing LMSs for the important work of the library: serving students and teachers. A centralized catalog will facilitate resource sharing among schools in our large district and leverage the existing wide area network investment of our MIS department. Information technology maintenance will be streamlined and have an interface with the district's student information system. This interface will also allow districtwide tracking of student reading statistics. School library media center staff will dedicate more time to educating students and assisting teachers rather than troubleshooting hardware and software.

OBJECTIVES

The objective of our vision for the future is to support student achievement. Whether by adding departmental personnel to lighten the paperwork load for LMSs or centralizing cataloging to relieve school personnel of backroom work and freeing them to work directly with students, the Department of Educational Media is supporting the district's goal to raise standards and increase academic achievement. A vital library program is possible only when the LMS is free to teach and interact with students and their teachers toward increasing academic achievement. A portion of the mission of the DeKalb County School System refers to the "management of all resources in an efficient, effective, and equitable manner." Certainly a centralized catalog will allow more efficient and effective management of the databases in every school for all students.

SCHOOL LIBRARY MEDIA SPECIALIST'S LEADERSHIP ROLE

DeKalb's LMSs will be responsible for preparing their databases for merger into a centralized database of MARC records with many holdings. At the system level, we will meet with vendors to compare the merits of their offerings. The MIS department of the school system is involved in order to guarantee the seamless interface of student information and other systems. This initiative was originated in the Department of Educational Media. The director, in addition to the five professional librarians in the department, has participated in joint Educational Media–MIS planning sessions. Departmental professionals are reviewing and evaluating the competing vendors' software, as has the DeKalb Teacher-Librarian Advisory council, a group of eight school LMSs elected by their peers. Their input, as the end users of such a system, is essential. Data will be maintained to evaluate effectiveness of the transition.

CONTRIBUTIONS TO STUDENT ACHIEVEMENT

Installation of the centralized catalog will do more than make information uniform from one school to the next; in addition, school LMSs will save valuable time for collaboration and teaching tasks. Full authority control will ensure uniform subject headings. Database entries will efficiently and uniformly direct students to appropriate materials. The system will allow keyword searching of the local school library collection as well as of all databases such as GALILEO (Georgia's web-based virtual library) and netTrekker.

FUNDING

The centralized catalog will cost $550,000 for installation, conversion, and a project manager to oversee operations. It will be funded by special project requests within the local system operating budget.

EVALUATION

Components supporting our vision and bringing it to reality may be evaluated by observation. Certainly departmental support contributes to the reduction in the duplication of work for 170 LMSs on a daily basis.

Collaboration Assessment and Library Use Continuum

KATHERINE LOWE
BOSTON ARTS ACADEMY/FENWAY HIGH SCHOOL LIBRARY AND BOSTON SYMPHONY ORCHESTRA EDUCATION RESOURCE CENTER, BOSTON, MASSACHUSETTS

I use the Collaboration Assessment and Library Use Continuum (exhibit 5.1) with individual classroom teachers or content teams at the conclusion of projects that we have planned together. First, I ask the teachers to make a list of the way they used the library space, resources, equipment, technology, and staff. Then we review the four levels of teamwork on the Library Use Continuum, defined as consumption, cooperation, coordination, and collaboration. I ask the teachers where they would place this project on the continuum and if they felt our collaboration was successful. This leads to a conversation in which we share ways we could have used our collective resources and expertise more effectively and determine how we can increase the depth of our collaboration in the future. Teachers appreciate this nonthreatening way to mutually reflect on our practice, and they begin to share my vision of what true collaboration is. I use this tool whenever I feel it is necessary to establish or reinforce my role in working collaboratively with classroom teachers.

Levels of Collaboration

Consumption
My students used the library to type and print their papers, print graphics, and/or construct their exhibition boards.

Cooperation
I informed the library staff about the project. The library staff provided resources for me and/or my students to use.

Coordination
I provided the library staff with content goals, expected product(s), due date, and assessment criteria for this project. I consulted with the library staff about the types of resources the students would use and the amount of time required in the library. The library staff taught my students how to access and use resources and assisted them with research.

Collaboration
A member of the library staff and I planned this project together. Time spent of this project in the library, the computer lab, and/or the classroom included learning experiences jointly taught with library staff. The library staff participated in assessing my students' work. Students' use of resources and their information literacy skills were assessed along with mastery of content.

Where would you place this project in the library use continuum?

Library Use Continuum

1	2	3	4
Consumption	Cooperation	Coordination	Collaboration

Source: Adapted from Sandra Hughes-Hassell and Anne Wheelock (eds.), *The Information-Powered School* (Chicago: American Library Association, 2001).

EXHIBIT 5.1

COLLABORATION ASSESSMENT AND LIBRARY USE CONTINUUM

Kapolei High School Library Media Center Vision and Action Plan

CAROLYN KIRIO
KAPOLEI HIGH SCHOOL LIBRARY MEDIA CENTER, KAPOLEI, HAWAII

SUMMARY

Kapolei High School was designed using a charrette process, the first high school in our state to do so. An invitation was extended to the community in 1998 to help develop the architectural components and curriculum of the school. All educational stakeholders were represented among the forty-nine individuals who accepted this invitation, including members of the educational field, neighboring businesses, and residents. Through months of planning and dialogue, a vision of the school was created that fueled the continued development of the school. This vision served as an inspiration for classroom design and is a constant directive for the selection and implementation of various teaching methodologies.

As a member of the charrette committee, I helped to create the vision of the school and currently serve as a curriculum leader who guides the school in its mission to fulfill this goal. The library then worked to develop its own vision of how the library can support the overall school objectives: "Kapolei High School Library is an exciting and dynamic learning environment which will provide research, curriculum, and technological support for every member of our learning community."

The media center has developed an array of services to support teaching and learning at the school as we fulfill this vision. These have included collaborative teaming with teachers to develop inquiry research lessons, project-based learning units, and senior project proposals.

OBJECTIVES

The library also incorporates the State Department of Education and Kapolei High School's mission within its own operational guidelines. Referred to as the "general learner outcomes," these attributes are characteristic of a successful high school graduate. Librarians assist students in acquiring these characteristics through meaningful, relevant lessons in support of the school's mission:

Kapolei High School creates opportunities for students to meet and exceed the Hawaii Content and Performance Standards. In addition, students will learn to

- ➤ be responsible for their own learning
- ➤ understand it is essential for people to work together
- ➤ be involved in complex thinking and problem solving
- ➤ recognize and produce quality performance and quality products
- ➤ be effective communicators
- ➤ be effective and ethical users of technology
- ➤ be global citizens who demonstrate caring, dignity, and integrity

SCHOOL LIBRARY MEDIA SPECIALIST'S LEADERSHIP ROLE

To meet the needs of their vision and mission, librarians have assumed diverse roles as information literacy specialists, curriculum leaders, and technology coordinators. Constant reflection on current services and practices identifies weaknesses and improvements. New knowledge and methods are in constant development, which supports the standards and teachers' efforts within the classroom.

EVALUATION

As part of the library's five-year action plan (exhibit 5.2), the librarians actively conduct program analysis and long-range planning. Yearly goals are developed to meet student and curriculum needs. The identified goals and elements are used to build the budget and support decisions regarding the acquisition of instructional materials. At the close of the school year, an in-depth analysis is conducted.[4] The results from this analysis are used to improve and refine library programs and services in support of the school and library's vision and mission.

Objective	Year 1	Year 2	Year 3	Year 4	Evaluation Completed	Objective Met
Collaboration, Leadership, and Technology *Become knowledgeable in and a leader for curriculum goals/initiatives* *Actively team and collaborate to integrate information literacy skills into the curriculum*	Collaborate with academies/ teams to develop standards-based lessons and assessments using rigor and relevance framework Facilitate develop curriculum maps with departments in alignment with HCPSIII Evaluate 2003 project- based learning cookbook and update areas for alignment with school initiatives	Continuous reevaluation of project-based learning cookbook and update areas for alignment with school initiatives Ongoing collaborative planning on rigor and relevance PBL lessons and assessments	Continuous reevaluation and update of project-based learning cookbook Ongoing collaborative planning on rigor and relevance PBL lessons Design and implement data gathering and assessment tools that measure the effectiveness/ impact of the library on student learning	Continuous reevaluation and update of project-based learning cookbook Ongoing collaborative planning on rigor and relevance PBL lessons Analyze and improve data gathering and assessment tools Reflect on and analyze data and make improvements that increase the effectiveness/ impact of the library on student learning		
Learning and Teaching *Students are engaged in reading, writing, speaking, viewing, and listening for enjoyment, enrichment, and understanding*	Analyze collection, acquire titles targeting reluctant/ emerging readers and publicize collection with school community Work with teachers to expand student literature reviews to increase literacy and promote collection Continue 2004 literacy efforts to encourage future reading consumers (i.e., book fairs, store)	Explore possibilities of online student reviews of literature Continue and explore alternate programs to encourage reading Update collection and web page ongoing	Implement online student reviews of literature Continue and explore alternate programs to encourage reading Update collection and web page ongoing	Continue program for online student reviews of literature Continue and explore alternate programs to encourage reading Update collection and web page ongoing		

EXHIBIT 5.2   KAPOLEI HIGH SCHOOL LIBRARY ACTION PLAN, 2005–2009

Objective	Year 1	Year 2	Year 3	Year 4	Evaluation Completed	Objective Met
Information Access and Delivery *Due to increased student population and possibility of multitrack schedule/ alternative education programs, access to library media center and its resources should be flexible and available both during and beyond the school day*	Explore expanding online databases and remote access of resources Reevaluate/ update procedure manual for changes in library operations due to multi-track/alternate education programs Continued development of K–12 complex procedure manual to reflect resource sharing between complex schools for increased access	Update KHS procedure manual/ development of complex procedure manuals ongoing Discuss with vendors online resources/ negotiate contracts if appropriate/ acquire funding	Update procedure manuals ongoing	Update procedure manuals ongoing		
Program Administration *Staffing enables the library media specialist to focus on collaborative curriculum development and other professional responsibilities while supervising staff performing nonprofessional library operations* *Library staff participates in ongoing professional development keeping abreast of trends/issues in library information and education*	Explore split-track scheduling/ alternate education program implications on library program administration/ services/staffing Evaluate staffing needs to support school initiatives (i.e., PBL, R&R framework, split-track, e-school) Librarians participate in conferences, workshops, etc., to keep current on trends	Outline budgetary concerns and update collection development to support school initiatives Librarians continue to participate in conferences, workshops, etc., to keep current on trends in education/ library information issues	Prepare for school initiatives Librarians continue to participate in conferences, workshops, etc., to keep current on trends in education/ library information issues	Possible implementation of school programs Librarians continue to participate in conferences, workshops, etc., to keep current on trends in education/ library information issues		

Objective	Year 1	Year 2	Year 3	Year 4	Evaluation Completed	Objective Met
Connection to the Learning Community *Explore avenues for expanding development/ recognition for "best practices" occurring at the school* *Librarians actively advocate the library program*	Explore and expand community partnerships for library support Develop/create alternative methods to promote library services and needs Continue attempts to gain national recognition for best practices	Continue attempts to gain national recognition for best practices Implement library advocacy materials to promote library services and needs	Continue attempts to gain national recognition for best practices Continue library advocacy	Continue attempts to gain national recognition for best practices Continue library advocacy		
Miscellaneous/ Other *Support the International Center for Leadership in Education's Rigor and Relevance Framework in schoolwide curriculum initiatives* *Learn, comprehend, and implement the new information literacy standards* *Analyze AYP data, devise and incorporate strategies within instruction to address the "gap population"*	Assist in strengthening rigorous and relevant in standards-based and project-based learning units/ lessons	Continue to provide curriculum assistance for staff development in professional learning communities	Continue to provide curriculum assistance in professional learning communities Reevaluate current initiatives and align/revise instruction to address new information literacy standards Analyze current AYP data collected through the administration of quarterly assessment tests	Continue to provide curriculum assistance in professional learning communities Evaluate and improve new information literacy standards instruction Develop teaching/ instructional strategies to address AYP data and incorporate methods within library skills instruction		

Present Assessment	Materials/ Resources Needed	Person(s) Involved/ Responsible and Expected Date of Completion
Collaboration process is in place but continually needs to be evaluated. Staff development time and planning time is needed to bring all academies/ teams online with standards-based lessons and assessments.	Staff development time Acquire adequate funding	*Curriculum Coordinator* *Librarians* *Technology Curriculum Coordinator* *Status - Ongoing* *Next Assessment: June 2008*
Ongoing collection development needs to be continued to meet the needs of reluctant and emerging readers. Expansion of literature reviews to include more teachers needed.	Acquire adequate funding Planning time	*Librarians* *Technology Curriculum Coordinator* *Status - Ongoing* *Next Assessment: June 2008*
Potential for special/off-campus educational opportunities will require alternative methods of information access and retrieval.	Acquire adequate funding Research time to study new information sources	*Librarians* *Technology Coordinator* *Status - Ongoing* *Next Assessment: June 2008*
Increase in school population will burden current library staff and resources. Adequate funding/ materials and staffing needs to be in place.	Acquire adequate funding Secure needed positions/staff	*Librarians* *Administration* *Status - Ongoing* *Next Assessment: June 2008*
While more effort has been made to publicize "best practices" occurring on campus, various accomplishments still need to be brought to the forefront.	Planning/composition time	*Librarians* *Status - Ongoing* *Next Assessment: June 2008*
Action plan to address 4 Rs has been implemented. Revisiting and evaluation needs to be completed to determine next course of action. Need to align practices with new information literacy standards.	Planning time	*Librarians* *Status - Ongoing* *Next Assessment: June 2008*

EXHIBIT 5.2 - CONTINUED

KAPOLEI HIGH SCHOOL LIBRARY ACTION PLAN, 2005–2009

Kapolei High School Vision

Kapolei High School is an exciting and dynamic student-centered learning environment at the heart of the community.

Kapolei High School Library Vision

Kapolei High School Library is an exciting and dynamic learning environment which will provide research, curriculum, and technological support for every member of our learning community.

Kapolei High School Mission

Kapolei High School will create opportunities for students to meet and exceed "The Hawaii Content and Performance Standards." In addition, students will learn to:

- ❑ Be responsible for their own learning
- ❑ Understand it is essential for people to work together
- ❑ Be involved in complex thinking and problem solving
- ❑ Recognize and produce quality performance and quality products
- ❑ Be effective communicators
- ❑ Be effective and ethical users of technology
- ❑ Be global citizens who demonstrate caring, dignity, and integrity

Curriculum "4 Rs"

Rigor

Kapolei High School's goal is for all students to exercise good communication, study skills, and work habits. The curriculum stresses high academic standards that allow students to exhibit mastery in different ways. Core competencies addressed schoolwide include analysis, reasoning, problem solving, collaboration, and teamwork. Learning challenges stimulate curiosity and discovery while engaging students in deeper questioning and investigation of topics, issues and situations. Construction of knowledge, and student performances/products reflect understanding at higher levels of thinking and successful application/ manipulation of information.

Relevance

Kapolei High School's curriculum allows students to see personal connections between the content being taught and experiences occurring within their own lives. Course work is challenging, and linked to students' interests as well as skills they will need as adults. Material being learned is applicable outside the school, challenges students with engaging real issues, and allows students to express student voice through personalized learning.

Relationships

Kapolei High School's educational environment fosters opportunities for students to learn from each other as well as with and from adults. Community internships, peer mentoring, service learning, and job shadowing provide valuable experiences from which bonds of trust and respect are formed. Hinged upon the establishment and maintenance of strong relationships, connections made bring relevance and realism to the academically rigorous curriculum.

Reflection

Kapolei High School's assessment process encourages the ongoing examination of acquired information, performance, and action by both students and teachers. Based upon evidence, options are considered and conscientious choices are made to diagnose problems, formulate solutions, and create strategies for improvement. Students and teachers who practice thoughtful evaluation build self-directed excellence which leads to lifelong learning and improvement.

EXHIBIT 5.2 - CONTINUED
KAPOLEI HIGH SCHOOL LIBRARY ACTION PLAN, 2005–2009

Ongoing Assessment for an Effective Library Program

PATRICIA PICKARD
DEKALB COUNTY SCHOOL SYSTEM, DECATUR, GEORGIA

SUMMARY

Ongoing assessment tools ensure that the library media program in the DeKalb County School System remains vital and effective in supporting students, teachers, and the curriculum. This ongoing assessment includes tools that assist the library media specialist (LMS) in identifying and evaluating program goals, reviewing job descriptions, and receiving support and feedback from the Department of Educational Media.

Our most effective assessment tools are

Library plan and goals: For many years, the Georgia State Department of Education, School Library Media Department, has required that each school prepare an annual library plan and goals. The DeKalb County School System's library media centers have traditionally completed these plans during the first semester so that the plan can be used as a road map during the school year. The Southern Associations of Colleges and Schools (SACS), the accrediting agency for schools in this area of the country, recently redirected its focus and began using the School Improvement Plan (SIP) as the instrument of choice. Under Standard 10, Continuous Process of School Improvement, each school has an improvement action plan containing priorities for improving student learning and school performances through the SACS accrediting process. In 2005, in an effort to align with the SIP, school library media specialists were asked to develop two library media program goals, each with a plan of action and a means of evaluation.

Consolidated School Improvement Plan: For the 2006 school year, the Department of Educational Media worked with the School Improvement Department to place the yearly Library Plan and Goals formally into the Consolidated School Improvement Plan (CSIP). The goal of the system is to have the entire school system undergo SACS review at the same time. The CSIP is the instrument that will be used throughout the system. The evolution of the Library Plan and Goals from development in isolation to inclusion in the CSIP shows that school LMSs are instructional leaders and team players in the school and that the library program makes a difference to student achievement.

Library media annual checklist: The library media annual checklist serves as a reminder of the many and varied duties and responsibilities of the LMS as outlined in standards and the expectations of the school system. School LMSs answer each question on the checklist by circling either yes or no, with a goal of all yes answers. There is space on the last page to give a brief explanation, rationale, time line for completion, or statement of concern, if applicable, for any no answers to questions that are not optional. With the required principal's signature on the final form submitted to the Department of Educational Media, LMSs are encouraged to use this opportunity to talk with their principals about what is happening in the library media center that will have a positive impact on student achievement.

Department of Educational Media support and feedback: The director and instructional coordinators are the administration and key players in responding to the needs of school LMSs. However, there are other team members (acquisitions secretary, district professional librarian, technology librarian, and librarian-at-large) who serve in unique positions to support the essential, priority work of the LMSs in the schools.

OBJECTIVES

The objectives of this best practice are to use tools that provide ongoing assessment of the library media program and align library media program goals with the CSIP. This best practice supports the system's goals because it is relevant, effective, and impacts student achievement.

SCHOOL LIBRARY MEDIA SPECIALIST'S LEADERSHIP ROLE

The Departmental of Educational Media takes the lead in planning, implementing, and evaluating the online assessment tools. The DeKalb Teacher-Librarian Advisory council, a group of eight school LMSs elected by their peers, advises the department on professional issues and serves as an internal advocacy group in promoting this and other best practices.

CONTRIBUTIONS TO STUDENT ACHIEVEMENT

The ongoing assessment tools provide the road map for the library media program; a checklist of program activities, duties, and responsibilities; and the identification of areas that need improvement. This best practice helps determine the effectiveness of the library program, which contributes to student achievement.

FUNDING

The ongoing assessment tools described are funded through the school district's ongoing budget with no additional external funds required.

EVALUATION

The director, coordinators, and other team members in the department review the goals and checklists submitted by the school library media specialists. Based on the information provided, LMSs receive feedback to correct problems or concerns with the goal of improved library media programs to support student achievement.

NOTES

1. Mary Alice Anderson, "Technician or Technologist," *Library Media Connection* 24, no. 1 (August–September 2005): 14.
2. Ibid.

3. *Wisconsin's Model Academic Standards for Information and Technology Literacy* (Madison, WI: Department of Public Instruction, 1998).

4. This analysis is conducted based on rubrics in *A Planning Guide for Information Power: Building Partnerships for Learning with School Library Media Program Assessment Rubric for the 21st Century* (Chicago: American Association of School Librarians, 1999).

postscript
Building NSLMPY-Worthy School Library Media Programs

School library media specialists who are committed to asking "Why?", who understand and embrace their multiple roles, who consistently communicate how the school library media center supports the needs of the school or district; who lead collaboration efforts, and who mold these actions into a vision for student learning create library media programs that are "instruments of school improvement."[1] An action plan for creating an exemplary school library is provided by Nance Nassar of the Colorado State Library through her "Ten Easy Leadership Ideas to Help School Librarians Become Leaders on Their Campus":

1. Meet regularly with your principal.
2. Attend all faculty meetings.
3. Serve on curriculum and standards committees.
4. Present professional development for teachers and librarians.
5. Engage in collaboration with teachers and technology staff.
6. Meet with school library colleagues.
7. Visit other school libraries.
8. Link to initiatives that are implemented on your campus and in your district.
9. Give recognition to others for your successes.
10. Attend and participate in district, state, and national association meetings and conferences.[2]

A commitment to reflection, collaboration, leadership, and technology to support dynamic, student-centered library media programs coupled with a commitment to action has enabled the leaders of the NSLMPY-recognized programs to provide a model for all those who are committed to student achievement.

NOTES

1. Gary Hartzell, "Why Should Principals Support School Libraries?" *ERIC Digest,* 2002. ERIC Document Reproduction Service ED470034, p. 2.

2. Presented by Keith Curry Lance at "Every Student Succeeds @ your library," 12th National Conference of the American Association of School Librarians, Pittsburgh, PA, October 6–9, 2005. Accessed August 1, 2007, at http://www.lrs.org/documents/lmcstudies/10_easy_ideas.pdf.

appendix

Websites of NSLMPY-Honored Programs

2008

LUELLA ELEMENTARY SCHOOL, LOCUST GROVE, GEORGIA (SINGLE SCHOOL)
http://schoolwires.henry.k12.ga.us/le/site/default.asp

SIMSBURY HIGH SCHOOL, SIMSBURY, CONNECTICUT (SINGLE SCHOOL)
http://simsbury.ccsct.com/page.cfm?p=43

2007

NORMAN, OKLAHOMA, PUBLIC SCHOOL DISTRICT, NORMAN, OKLAHOMA (SCHOOL DISTRICT)
http://www.norman.k12.ok.us/misc/library/

HARPETH HIGH SCHOOL, KINGSTON SPRING, TENNESSEE (SINGLE SCHOOL)
http://www.cheathamcountytracs.com/harpeth_high_school.htm

NORTH ELEMENTARY SCHOOL, NOBLESVILLE, INDIANA (SINGLE SCHOOL)
http://www.noblesvilleschools.org/nobln.nsf/LESSDATE?OpenView&id=70222006

2006

HILLIARD CITY SCHOOL DISTRICT, HILLIARD, OHIO (SCHOOL DISTRICT)
http://www.hilliardschools.org/departments/currESMedia.cfm

BIBLIOTECA LAS AMERICAS, MERCEDES, TEXAS (SINGLE SCHOOL)
http://bla.stisd.net

KAPOLEI HIGH SCHOOL, KAPOLEI, HAWAII (SINGLE SCHOOL)
http://www.k12.hi.us/%7Ekaphlib/

2005

WILLIAM FLOYD SCHOOL DISTRICT, MASTIC BEACH, NEW YORK (LARGE DISTRICT)
http://www.wfsd.k12.ny.us/departments/library.asp

DOWNERS GROVE SOUTH HIGH SCHOOL, DOWNERS GROVE, ILLINOIS (TIE; SINGLE SCHOOL)
http://bb.csd99.org/webapps/portal/frameset.jsp?tab_id=_44_1

HENRY BRADER ELEMENTARY SCHOOL, NEWARK, DELAWARE (TIE; SINGLE SCHOOL)
http://www.christina.k12.de.us/brader/Library/index.htm

2004

NORTHSIDE INDEPENDENT SCHOOL DISTRICT, SAN ANTONIO, TEXAS (LARGE DISTRICT)
http://www.nisd.net/libww/Adobe/LIBRARY%20MEDIA%20BEST%20PRACTICES.ppt
OR http://209.85.135.104/custom?q=cache:hHLLXE9k5PgJ:www.nisd.net/libww/Adobe/L
IBRARY%2520MEDIA%2520BEST%2520PRACTICES.ppt+NSLMPY&hl=en&ct=clnk
&cd=1&gl=us&client=google-coop-np

BOSTON ARTS ACADEMY/FENWAY HIGH SCHOOL, BOSTON, MASSACHUSETTS (TIE; SINGLE
SCHOOL)
http://fenway.boston.k12.ma.us/library/index.htm

LOIS LENSKI ELEMENTARY SCHOOL, LITTLETON, COLORADO (TIE; SINGLE SCHOOL)
http://lenski.littletonpublicschools.net

2003

MILLARD PUBLIC SCHOOL DISTRICT, OMAHA, NEBRASKA (LARGE DISTRICT)
http://www.mpsomaha.org/mnhs/academics/Mediacenter/mediaindex.htm

LIBERTY PUBLIC SCHOOL DISTRICT, LIBERTY, MISSOURI (SMALL DISTRICT)
http://liberty.k12.mo.us/TeachingLearning/Library.php

CHERRY CREEK HIGH SCHOOL, GREENWOOD VILLAGE, COLORADO (SINGLE SCHOOL)
http://www.cchs.ccsd.k12.co.us/lib_res/lib_res.html

2002

JAMES RIVER HIGH SCHOOL, MIDLOTHIAN, VIRGINIA (SINGLE SCHOOL)
http://jrhs.ccpsnet.net/library_index.php

2001

DEKALB COUNTY SCHOOL SYSTEM, DECATUR, GEORGIA (LARGE DISTRICT)
http://www.dekalb.k12.ga.us/instruction/edmedia/index.html

CORBETT ELEMENTARY SCHOOL, TUCSON, ARIZONA (SINGLE SCHOOL)
http://edweb.tusd.k12.az.us/corbettlibrary/

2000

IRVING INDEPENDENT SCHOOL DISTRICT, IRVING, TEXAS (LARGE DISTRICT)
http://www.youseemore.com/IrvingSchool/default.asp

LONDONDERRY SCHOOL DISTRICT #12, LONDONDERRY, NEW HAMPSHIRE (SMALL DISTRICT)
http://www.londonderry.org/lmt/index.cfm

NEW TRIER TOWNSHIP HIGH SCHOOL, WINNETKA, ILLINOIS (SINGLE SCHOOL)
http://www.newtrier.k12.il.us/library/default.htm

1999

LINCOLN PUBLIC SCHOOLS, LINCOLN, NEBRASKA (LARGE DISTRICT)
http://sites.lps.org/lms/

1998

HUNTERDON CENTRAL REGIONAL HIGH SCHOOL, FLEMINGTON, NEW JERSEY (SINGLE SCHOOL)
http://central.hcrhs.k12.nj.us/imc/

1997

GWINNETT COUNTY PUBLIC SCHOOLS, SUWANNEE, GEORGIA (LARGE DISTRICT)
http://www.gwinnett.k12.ga.us/gcps-mainweb01.nsf/pages/GCPSHome0~MainPage

IOWA CITY COMMUNITY SCHOOL DISTRICT, IOWA CITY, IOWA (SMALL DISTRICT)
http://www.iowa-city.k12.ia.us/Library/

TIMOTHY DWIGHT ELEMENTARY SCHOOL, FAIRFIELD, CONNECTICUT (SINGLE SCHOOL)
https://www.edline.net/pages/DWIGHT_ELEMENTARY_SCHOOL/Virtual_Library/

1996

MAINE TOWNSHIP HIGH SCHOOL WEST, DES PLAINES, ILLINOIS (SINGLE SCHOOL)
http://webpages.maine207.org/west/departments/lrc/index.html

1995

SOUTHERN BLUFFS ELEMENTARY SCHOOL, LA CROSSE, WISCONSIN (SINGLE SCHOOL)
http://www.rschooltoday.com/se3bin/clientgenie.cgi

SMOKY HILL HIGH SCHOOL, AURORA, COLORADO (SINGLE SCHOOL)
http://www.smoky.ccsd.k12.co.us/

1994

DUNELAND SCHOOL CORPORATION, CHESTERTON, INDIANA (SMALL DISTRICT)
http://www.duneland.k12.in.us/programs/mediatech/start/awards.html

PROVIDENCE SENIOR HIGH SCHOOL, CHARLOTTE, NORTH CAROLINA (SINGLE SCHOOL)
http://pages.cms.k12.nc.us/providencemedia/

LAKEVIEW ELEMENTARY SCHOOL, NEENAH, WISCONSIN (SINGLE SCHOOL)
http://www.neenah.k12.wi.us/lv/

1993

BLUE VALLEY SCHOOL DISTRICT USD 229, OVERLAND PARK, KANSAS (LARGE DISTRICT)
http://education.bluevalleyk12.org/bvlmc/aboutthelibrary.cfm

INDIAN PRAIRIE SCHOOL DISTRICT 204, NAPERVILLE, ILLINOIS (SMALL DISTRICT)
http://nvhs.ipsd.org/lmc.asp

1992

FULTON COUNTY SCHOOL SYSTEM, ATLANTA, GEORGIA (LARGE DISTRICT)
http://www2.fultonschools.org/dept/medsvcs/

MANHATTAN/OGDEN UNIFIED SCHOOL DISTRICT 383, MANHATTAN, KANSAS
(SMALL DISTRICT)
http://www.usd383.org/Schools/Secondary/MHS/Academics/LibraryMediaCenter.aspx

1991

IRVING INDEPENDENT SCHOOL DISTRICT, IRVING, TEXAS (LARGE DISTRICT)
http://www.youseemore.com/IrvingSchool/default.asp

BEECHER ROAD SCHOOL, WOODBRIDGE, CONNECTICUT (SINGLE SCHOOL)
http://www.woodbridgesd.org/curriculum_library_tech.html

1990

GREENSBORO PUBLIC SCHOOLS, GREENSBORO, NORTH CAROLINA (LARGE DISTRICT)
http://www.gcsnc.com/depts/library_media_services/index.html (the district name changed to Guilford County Schools in 1992)

CHERRY CREEK HIGH SCHOOL, GREENWOOD VILLAGE, COLORADO (SINGLE SCHOOL)
http://www.cchs.ccsd.k12.co.us/lib_res/lib_res.html

1989

NORMAN PUBLIC SCHOOLS, NORMAN, OKLAHOMA (LARGE DISTRICT)
http://www.norman.k12.ok.us/misc/library/

MIDDLETOWN ENLARGED CITY SCHOOL DISTRICT, MIDDLETOWN, NEW YORK (SMALL DISTRICT)
http://www.middletowncityschools.org/default.htm

DAVID A. HICKMAN HIGH SCHOOL, COLUMBIA, MISSOURI (SINGLE SCHOOL)
http://www.columbia.k12.mo.us/hhs/mc/mediacenter03/databases.htm

1988

WEST BLOOMFIELD SCHOOLS, WEST BLOOMFIELD, MICHIGAN (LARGE DISTRICT)
http://www.westbloomfield.k12.mi.us

ROUND ROCK INDEPENDENT SCHOOL DISTRICT, ROUND ROCK, TEXAS (SMALL DISTRICT)
https://www.roundrockisd.org/home/index.asp?page=393

1987

INDEPENDENT SCHOOL DISTRICT 47, SAUK RAPIDS, MINNESOTA (LARGE DISTRICT)
http://www.isd47.org/schools/saukrapids-ricehighschool/mediacenter/index.php

COMMUNITY CONSOLIDATED SCHOOL DISTRICT 62, DES PLAINES, ILLINOIS (SMALL DISTRICT)
http://www.d62.org/home/index.html

MONTEREY PENINSULA UNIFIED SCHOOL DISTRICT, MONTEREY, CALIFORNIA (SCHOOL)
http://www.youseemore.com/MPUSD/school.asp?schooltype=ms&branch=7100

1986

DISTRICT 108, HIGHLAND PARK, ILLINOIS
http://www.pekin.net/pekin108/contribute/jdarnell/WashingtonLearningCenter.html

1985

SHOREHAM-WADING RIVER SCHOOL DISTRICT, SHOREHAM, NEW YORK
http://www.swrcsd.org/schools/swrhs_database.asp

1984

RIVERSIDE-BROOKFIELD TOWNSHIP HIGH SCHOOL, RIVERSIDE, ILLINOIS
http://www.rbhs208.org/LITFINAL/Lithome.htm

RICHMOND SCHOOL SYSTEM, RICHMOND, VIRGINIA
http://www.richmond.k12.va.us/schools/jefferson_new/departments/media.cfm

1983

No award given

1982

SHAKER HEIGHTS CITY SCHOOL DISTRICT, SHAKER HEIGHTS, OHIO
http://www.shaker.org/resources/library/

1981

BLUE VALLEY SCHOOL DISTRICT, SHAWNEE MISSION, KANSAS
http://education.bluevalleyk12.org/bvlmc/

1980

IRVINE UNIFIED SCHOOL DISTRICT, IRVINE, CALIFORNIA
http://www.iusd.org/uhs/new/mediacenter/2ndtry.html

1979

GREENWICH PUBLIC SCHOOLS, GREENWICH, CONNECTICUT
http://www.greenwichschools.org/page.cfm?p=888

1978

COBB COUNTY PUBLIC SCHOOLS, MARIETTA, GEORGIA
http://cvl.cobbk12.org

1977

LOS ALAMITOS SCHOOL DISTRICT, LOS ALAMITOS, CALIFORNIA
http://losal.schoolwires.com/losal/site/default.asp

1976

LITTLETON PUBLIC SCHOOLS, LITTLETON, COLORADO
http://www.littletonpublicschools.net

1975

ROCHESTER CITY SCHOOLS, ROCHESTER, NEW YORK
http://rochestersls.rcsdk12.org

1974

CEDAR RAPIDS COMMUNITY SCHOOLS, CEDAR RAPIDS, IOWA
http://intranet.cr.k12.ia.us/media/index.html

1973

DUNELAND COMMUNITY SCHOOLS, CHESTERTON, INDIANA
http://www.duneland.k12.in.us/programs/mediatech/mediatech.html

1972

ATLANTA PUBLIC SCHOOLS, ATLANTA, GEORGIA
http://www.atlanta.k12.ga.us/content/apshome.aspx

1971

LEFLORE COUNTY SCHOOLS, GREENWOOD, MISSISSIPPI
http://www.leflorecountyschools.org/index.html

1970

ALHAMBRA SCHOOL DISTRACT, PHOENIX, ARIZONA
http://www.alhambra.k12.az.us/schools.html

1969

IOWA CITY COMMUNITY SCHOOLS, IOWA CITY, IOWA
http://www.iowa-city.k12.ia.us/NEWINFO/LibMedia.html

1968

SAN RAMON VALLEY SCHOOL DISTRICT, DANVILLE, CALIFORNIA
http://www.srvusd.k12.ca.us/Schools/Library_Media_Centers/

1967

CLEVELAND PUBLIC SCHOOLS, CLEVELAND, OHIO
http://www.cmsdnet.net/CMSDintro.htm (the district name changed to Cleveland Metropolitan School District in 2007)

1966

ALBUQUERQUE PUBLIC SCHOOLS, ALBUQUERQUE, NEW MEXICO
http://www.aps.edu/aps/libraryservices/main.html

1965

DADE COUNTY PUBLIC SCHOOLS, MIAMI, FLORIDA
http://it.dadeschools.net/library/index.htm

1964

DURHAM COUNTY SCHOOLS, DURHAM, NORTH CAROLINA
http://www.dpsnc.net (the district name changed to Durham Public Schools, n.d.)

1963

ANNE ARUNDEL COUNTY SCHOOLS, ANNAPOLIS, MARYLAND
http://www.aacps.org/lms/

bibliography

Resources for Exemplary
School Library Media Programs

American Association of School Librarians, Association for Educational Communications and Technology. *Information Power: Building Partnerships for Learning.* Chicago: American Library Association, 1998.

———. *A Planning Guide for Information Power: Building Partnerships for Learning with School Library Media Program Assessment Rubric for the 21st Century.* Chicago: American Library Association, 1999.

Andronik, Catherine, ed. *School Library Management,* 5th ed. Worthington, OH: Linworth Publishing, 2003.

Erikson, Rolf, and Carolyn Markuson. *Designing a School Library Media Center for the Future.* Chicago: American Library Association, 2001.

Farmer, Lesley S. J. *Teaming with Opportunity: Media Programs, Community Constituencies, and Technology.* Englewood, CO: Libraries Unlimited, 2001.

Hartzell, Gary. "Why Should Principals Support School Libraries?" *ERIC Digest,* 2002. ERIC Documentation Reproduction Service ED470034. Available on the Internet at http://www.eric.ed.gov/ERICDocs/data/ericdocs2sql/content_storage_01/0000019b/80/1a/84/84.pdf.

Lance, Keith Curry. *The Impact of School Library Media Centers on Academic Achievement.* Prepared for the U.S. Department of Education, Office of Educational Research and Improvement Library Programs. Denver: Colorado Department of Education, 1993. (See also *School Library Impact Studies* for additional studies. Available on the Internet at http://www.lrs.org/impact.php.)

Lankford, Mary. *Leadership and the School Librarian: Essays from Leaders in the Field.* Worthington, OH: Linworth Publishing, 2006.

"Library Power Program Evaluation." Special issue of *School Libraries Worldwide* 5, no. 2 (July 1999).

Loertscher, David V. *Taxonomies of the School Library Media Program,* 2nd ed. San Jose, CA: Hi Willow Press, 2000.

Loertscher, David V., and Ross J. Todd. *We Boost Achievement: Evidence-Based Practice for School Library Media Specialists.* Salt Lake City, UT: Hi Willow Research and Publishing, 2003.

The White House Conference on School Libraries Proceedings, June 4, 2002. Washington, DC: Institute on Museum and Library Services, 2002. ERIC Documentation Reproduction Service ED472595.

Wilson, Patricia Potter, and Josette Anne Lyders. *Leadership for Today's School Library: A Handbook for the School Library Media Specialist and the School Principal.* Westport, CT: Greenwood Press, 2001.

contributors

SUSIE ALEXANDER *Hilliard City School District, Hilliard, Ohio*

STEPHANIE BEISCH *Millard South High School, Omaha, Nebraska*

SHARON BRUBAKER *H. M. Brader Elementary School, Newark, Delaware*

ANGELA BURNS *New Trier High School, Winnetka, Illinois*

MARILYN COBB *New Trier High School, Winnetka, Illinois*

SHARON COIL *Cherry Creek High School, Greenwood Village, Colorado*

LIZ DESKINS *Hilliard City School District, Hilliard, Ohio*

CHRISTINA H. DORR, PH.D. *Hilliard City School District, Hilliard, Ohio*

JUDY GRESSEL *New Trier High School, Northfield, Illinois*

DONNA HELVERING *Millard Public Schools, Omaha, Nebraska*

JULIE HYDE-PORTER *Cherry Creek High School, Greenwood Village, Colorado*

CAROLYN KIRIO *Kapolei High School, Kapolei, Hawaii*

JANIE KOSSAK *Austin Elementary School, DeKalb County School System, Dunwoody, Georgia*

TERRY LORD *Hilliard City School District, Hilliard, Ohio*

KATHERINE LOWE *Boston Arts Academy/Fenway High School Library and Boston Symphony Orchestra Education Resource Center, Boston, Massachusetts*

KRISTIN MCKEOWN *Cherry Creek High School, Greenwood Village, Colorado*

ANNA MARIA MENZA *Cherry Creek High School, Greenwood Village, Colorado*

ANNE O'MALLEY *New Trier High School, Northfield, Illinois*

MARSHA PFAHL *Hilliard City School District, Hilliard, Ohio*

PATRICIA PICKARD *DeKalb County School System, Decatur, Georgia*

MAGGIE SCHMUDE *New Trier High School, Winnetka, Illinois*

PAM STROM *New Trier High School, Winnetka, Illinois*

DIANE H. THOMPSON *Cherry Creek High School, Greenwood Village, Colorado*

MARY TRENERRY *Millard Public Schools, Omaha, Nebraska*

index